THE NEW FOLGER LIBRARY SHAKESPEARE

Designed to make Shakespeare's great plays available to all readers, the New Folger Library edition of Shakespeare's plays provides accurate texts in modern spelling and punctuation, as well as scene-by-scene action summaries, full explanatory notes, many pictures clarifying Shakespeare's language, and notes recording all significant departures from the early printed versions. Each play is prefaced by a brief introduction, by a guide to reading Shakespeare's language, and by accounts of his life and theater. Each play is followed by an annotated list of further readings and by a "Modern Perspective" written by an expert on that particular play.

Barbara A. Mowat is Director of Academic Programs at the Folger Shakespeare Library, Executive Editor of *Shakespeare Quarterly*, Chair of the Folger Institute, and author of *The Dramaturgy of Shakespeare's Romances* and of essays on Shakespeare's plays and on the editing of the plays.

Paul Werstine is Professor of English at the Graduate School and at King's University College at the University of Western Ontario. He is general editor of the New Variorum Shakespeare and author of many papers and articles on the printing and editing of Shakespeare's plays.

The Folger Shakespeare Library

The Folger Shakespeare Library in Washington, D.C., a privately funded research library dedicated to Shakespeare and the civilization of early modern Europe, was founded in 1932 by Henry Clay and Emily Jordan Folger. In addition to its role as the world's preeminent Shakespeare collection and its emergence as a leading center for Renaissance studies, the Folger Library offers a wide array of cultural and educational programs and services for the general public.

EDITORS

BARBARA A. MOWAT
Director of Academic Programs
Folger Shakespeare Library

PAUL WERSTINE
Professor of English
King's University College at the University of
Western Ontario, Canada

FOLGER SHAKESPEARE LIBRARY

A Midsummer Night's Dream

By
WILLIAM SHAKESPEARE

EDITED BY BARBARA A. MOWAT
AND PAUL WERSTINE

WASHINGTON SQUARE PRESS
New York London Toronto Sydney

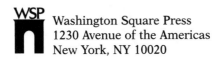 Washington Square Press
1230 Avenue of the Americas
New York, NY 10020

ISBN: 0-7434-8281-6

First Washington Square Press New Folger Trade Paperback
Edition November 1999
This Edition August 2004

10 9 8 7 6 5 4 3 2 1

For information regarding special discounts for bulk
purchases, please contact Simon & Schuster Special Sales
at 1-800-456-6798 or business@simonandschuster.com.

From the Director of the Library

For over four decades, the Folger Library General Reader's Shakespeare provided accurate and accessible texts of the plays and poems to students, teachers, and millions of other interested readers. Today, in an age often impatient with the past, the passion for Shakespeare continues to grow. No author speaks more powerfully to the human condition, in all its variety, than this actor/playwright from a minor sixteenth-century English village.

Over the years vast changes have occurred in the way Shakespeare's works are edited, performed, studied, and taught. The New Folger Library Shakespeare replaces the earlier versions, bringing to bear the best and most current thinking concerning both the texts and their interpretation. Here is an edition which makes the plays and poems fully understandable for modern readers using uncompromising scholarship. Professors Barbara Mowat and Paul Werstine are uniquely qualified to produce this New Folger Shakespeare for a new generation of readers. The Library is grateful for the learning, clarity, and imagination they have brought to this ambitious project.

Werner Gundersheimer,
Director of the Folger Shakespeare Library
from 1984 to 2002

Contents

Editors' Preface   *ix*

Shakespeare's *A Midsummer Night's Dream*   *xiii*

Reading Shakespeare's Language   *xiv*

Shakespeare's Life   *xxviii*

Shakespeare's Theater   *xxxvi*

The Publication of Shakespeare's Plays   *xliv*

An Introduction to This Text   *xlviii*

A Midsummer Night's Dream
   Text of the Play with Commentary   *1*

Textual Notes   *175*

A Midsummer Night's Dream: **A Modern**
   Perspective, by Catherine Belsey   *181*

Further Reading   *191*

Key to Famous Lines and Phrases   *203*

Editors' Preface

In recent years, ways of dealing with Shakespeare's texts and with the interpretation of his plays have been undergoing significant change. This edition, while retaining many of the features that have always made the Folger Shakespeare so attractive to the general reader, at the same time reflects these current ways of thinking about Shakespeare. For example, modern readers, actors, and teachers have become interested in the differences between, on the one hand, the early forms in which Shakespeare's plays were first published and, on the other hand, the forms in which editors through the centuries have presented them. In response to this interest, we have based our edition on what we consider the best early printed version of a particular play (explaining our rationale in a section called "An Introduction to This Text") and have marked our changes in the text—unobtrusively, we hope, but in such a way that the curious reader can be aware that a change has been made and can consult the "Textual Notes" to discover what appeared in the early printed version.

Current ways of looking at the plays are reflected in our brief introductions, in many of the commentary notes, in the annotated lists of "Further Reading," and especially in each play's "Modern Perspective," an essay written by an outstanding scholar who brings to the reader his or her fresh assessment of the play in the light of today's interests and concerns.

As in the Folger Library General Reader's Shakespeare, which this edition replaces, we include explanatory notes designed to help make Shakespeare's language clearer to a modern reader, and we place the notes on the page facing the text that they explain. We also follow the earlier edition in including illustrations —of objects, of clothing, of mythological figures—from books and manuscripts in the Folger Library collection. We provide fresh accounts of the life of Shakespeare, of the publishing of his plays, and of the theaters in which his plays were performed, as well as an introduction to the text itself. We also include a section called "Reading Shakespeare's Language," in which we try to help readers learn to "break the code" of Elizabethan poetic language.

For each section of each volume, we are indebted to a host of generous experts and fellow scholars. The "Reading Shakespeare's Language" sections, for example, could not have been written had not Arthur King, of Brigham Young University, and Randal Robinson, author of *Unlocking Shakespeare's Language,* led the way in untangling Shakespearean language puzzles and shared their insights and methodologies generously with us. "Shakespeare's Life" profited by the careful reading given it by S. Schoenbaum, "Shakespeare's Theater" was read and strengthened by Andrew Gurr and John Astington, and "The Publication of Shakespeare's Plays" is indebted to the comments of Peter W. M. Blayney. We, as editors, take sole responsibility for any errors in our editions.

We are grateful to the authors of the "Modern Perspectives," to Leeds Barroll and David Bevington for their generous encouragement, to the Huntington and Newberry Libraries for fellowship support, to King's College for the grants it has provided to Paul Werstine, to the Social Sciences and Humanities Research Council of Canada, which provided him with a Research Time Stipend for 1990–91, and to the Folger Institute's Center for Shakespeare Studies for its fortuitous sponsorship of a workshop on "Shakespeare's Texts for Students and

Teachers" (funded by the National Endowment for the Humanities and led by Richard Knowles of the University of Wisconsin), a workshop from which we learned an enormous amount about what is wanted by college and high-school teachers of Shakespeare today.

Our biggest debt is to the Folger Shakespeare Library: to Werner Gundersheimer, Director of the Library, who has made possible our edition; to Jean Miller, the Library's Art Curator, who combed the Library holdings for illustrations, and to Julie Ainsworth, Head of the Photography Department, who carefully photographed them; to Peggy O'Brien, Director of Education, who gave us expert advice about the needs being expressed by Shakespeare teachers and students (and to Martha Christian and other "master teachers" who used our texts in manuscript in their classrooms); to the staff of the Academic Programs Division, especially Paul Menzer (who drafted "Further Reading" material), Mary Tonkinson, Lena Cowen Orlin, Molly Haws, and Jessica Hymowitz; and, finally, to the staff of the Library Reading Room, whose patience and support have been invaluable.

Barbara A. Mowat and Paul Werstine

Shakespeare's
A Midsummer Night's Dream

In *A Midsummer Night's Dream,* Shakespeare confronts us with mysterious images of romantic desire. There are Theseus and Hippolyta, about to be married; both are strange and wonderful figures from classical mythology. Theseus is a great warrior, a kinsman of Hercules; she is an Amazon, a warrior-woman, defeated in battle by Theseus. His longing for the wedding day opens the play, and the play closes with their exit to their marriage bed.

Within Theseus's world of Athens, two young men and two young women sort themselves out into marriageable couples, but only after one triangle, with Hermia at the apex and Helena excluded, is temporarily replaced by another, this time with Helena at the apex and Hermia excluded. At each point the fickle young men think they are behaving rationally and responsibly as infatuation (sometimes caused by a magic flower, sometimes not) leads them into fierce claims and counterclaims, and the audience is shown the power of desire to take over one's vision and one's actions. By presenting the young lovers as almost interchangeable, Shakespeare displays and probes the mystery of how lovers find differences—compelling, life-shaping differences—where there seem to be only likenesses.

In the woods outside of Athens, where the lovers suffer their strange love experiences, we find yet other images of desire, these involving the king and queen of Fairyland and an Athenian weaver transformed into an ass-headed monster. King Oberon and Queen Titania are engaged in a near-epic battle over custody of an orphan boy; the king uses magic to make the queen fall in love with the monster. The monster—a simple weaver named Bottom who came into the woods with his companions to rehearse a play for Theseus and Hippolyta's wedding—is himself the victim of magic. He has been turned into a monster by Oberon's helper, a hobgoblin or "puck" named Robin Goodfellow. The love-experience of Titania and Bottom is a playing out of the familiar "beauty and the beast" story, and, like the stories of the young lovers, it makes us wonder at the power of infatuation to transform the image of the beloved in the lover's eyes.

Finally, there is the tragic love story of "Pyramus and Thisbe," ineptly written and staged by Bottom and his workingmen companions. In this story romantic love leads to a double suicide—provoking only mirth in the onstage audience but reminding us once again of the extraordinary power of desire.

In *A Midsummer Night's Dream,* one of Shakespeare's most popular plays, Shakespeare stages the workings of love in ways that have fascinated generations of playgoers and readers. After you have read the play, we invite you to read "A Modern Perspective" on *A Midsummer Night's Dream* written by Professor Catherine Belsey of Cardiff University, printed at the back of this book.

Reading Shakespeare's Language

For many people today, reading Shakespeare's language can be a problem—but it is a problem that can be solved. Those who have studied Latin (or even French or German or Spanish) and those who are used to reading poetry will have little difficulty understanding the language of Shakespeare's poetic drama. Others, though, need to develop the skills of untangling unusual sentence structures and of recognizing and understanding poetic compressions, omissions, and wordplay. And even those skilled in reading unusual sentence structures may have occasional trouble with Shakespeare's words. Four hundred years of "static" intervene between his speaking and our hearing. Most of his immense vocabulary is still in use, but a few of his words are not, and, worse, some of his words now have meanings quite different from those they had in the sixteenth century. In the theater, most of these difficulties are solved for us by actors who study the language and articulate it for us so that the essential meaning is heard—or, when combined with stage action, is at least *felt*. When reading on one's own, one must do what each actor does: go over the lines (often with a dictionary close at hand) until the puzzles are solved and the lines yield up their poetry and the characters speak in words and phrases that are, suddenly, rewarding and wonderfully memorable.

Shakespeare's Words

As you begin to read the opening scenes of a play by Shakespeare, you may notice occasional unfamiliar words. Some are unfamiliar simply because we no longer use them. In the opening scenes of *A Midsummer Night's Dream*, for example, you will find the words *mewed* (i.e., caged), *an* (i.e., if), *beteem* (i.e., grant, give), *momentany* (i.e., momentary), and *collied* (i.e., coal black). Words of this kind are explained in notes to the text and will become familiar the more of Shakespeare's plays you read.

In *A Midsummer Night's Dream*, as in all of Shakespeare's writing, more problematic than discarded words are words that we still use but that we use with a different meaning. In the opening scene of *A Midsummer Night's Dream*, for example, the word *conceit* has the meaning of "a fancy trinket," the word *solemnity* is used where we would say "festive ceremony," *blood* where we would say "passions, feelings," *fantasy* where we would say "imagination," and *well possessed* where we would say "wealthy." Such words will be explained in the notes to the text, but they, too, will become familiar as you continue to read Shakespeare's language.

Some words are strange not because of the "static" introduced by changes in language over the past centuries but because these are words that Shakespeare is using to build a dramatic world that has its own space, time, history, and background mythology. *A Midsummer Night's Dream* is a particularly interesting example of this practice in that, in this play, Shakespeare creates three such worlds, each of which thinly veils other, very different worlds. In the play's first scene he builds a world that purports to be the city of Athens, home to the legendary characters Theseus and Hippolyta. That world exists in references to "Athenian youth," to "the law of Athens," and to "Athens' gates." But the language used in this Athens creates not a recognizable Greek city (in contrast to the opening scenes of, say, *Julius Caesar*, where the language creates a Rome of the classic past) but rather a placeless, almost timeless world of romantic love, of ritual, of mythology. This romance world is created through references to May Day "observances," to "Diana's altar," to "Venus' doves," to "winged Cupid," to "Cupid's strongest bow," and to "his best arrow with the golden head."

In the play's second scene, Shakespeare builds a world of supposedly Athenian workingmen (a world created primarily through the names of the men's occupations—joiner, bellows-mender, tinker) but here again language displaces this world and creates a world of theater, with its "scrolls," "scrips," "parts," "cues," and "bills of properties." References to mythological figures appear here, as they do in the world of Theseus's Athens, but now transformed through the language of the uneducated workers into comic references to "Phibbus' car" (i.e., the chariot of the sun god, Phoebus) and to "Ercles" (i.e., Hercules).

Finally, in the play's third scene, he creates the world of Fairyland, ruled over by Oberon, king of the fairies, and Titania, his queen. This world is made through references to "changelings," to "fairy ringlets" (i.e., circle dances), to "orbs" (i.e., the dancing ground of fairies), and to such magic flowers as "love-in-idleness." But more interesting are the other worlds created through the language of the fairies—first, the world of English country villagers affected by the doings of fairies, especially by that "lob of sprites," Robin Goodfellow, a world that is never shown onstage but that is created through references to the "villagery," the "quern," the "gossips' bowl," the old "aunt" with her "withered dewlap," the "quaint mazes in the wanton green," the "murrain flock," and "nine-men's-morris"; second, the world of Titania's past, with its mortal "vot'ress" who sat with her in the "spicèd Indian air" on "Neptune's yellow sands," watching "embarkèd traders on the flood"; and, third, the world of Oberon's past, with its "mermaid on a dolphin's back," its "bolt of Cupid," its "vestal thronèd by the West." This pattern of displacement, this creation of worlds that thinly veil quite different worlds, may well help to explain this play's magic, otherworldly quality.

Shakespeare's Sentences

In an English sentence, meaning is quite dependent on the place given each word. "The dog bit the boy" and "The boy bit the dog" mean very different things, even though the individual words are the same. Because English places such importance on the positions of words in sentences, on the way words are arranged, unusual arrangements can puzzle a reader. Shakespeare frequently shifts his sentences away from "normal" English arrangements—often to create the rhythm he seeks, sometimes to use a line's poetic rhythm to emphasize a particular word, sometimes to give a character his or her own speech patterns or to allow the character to speak in a special way. Again, when we attend a good performance of the play, the actors will have worked out the sentence structures and will articulate the sentences so that the meaning is clear. In reading for yourself, do as the actor does. That is, when you become puzzled by a character's speech, check to see if words are being presented in an unusual sequence.

Look first for the placement of subject and verb. Shakespeare often places the verb before the subject (e.g., instead of "He goes," we find "Goes he"). In *A Midsummer Night's Dream,* we find such a construction when Egeus says (1.1.23) "Full of vexation come I" (instead of "Full of vexation I come"); Lysander uses this same kind of construction when, at 1.1.163, he says "There, gentle Hermia, *may I* marry thee," as does Hermia at 1.1.209–10, when she says "Before the time I did Lysander see / *Seemed Athens* as a paradise to me." Helena's "But herein *mean I* to enrich my pain" (1.1.256) is another example of inverted subject and verb.

Such inversions rarely cause much confusion. More

problematic is Shakespeare's frequent placing of the object before the subject and verb (e.g., instead of "I hit him," we might find "Him I hit"). Egeus's "And what is mine my love shall render him" (1.1.98) is an example of such an inversion (the normal order would be "And my love shall render him what is mine"), as is Helena's "Things base and vile, holding no quantity, / Love can transpose to form and dignity" (1.1.238–39), where "things base and vile" is the object of the verb "transpose."

Inversions are not the only unusual sentence structures in Shakespeare's language. Often in his sentences words that would normally appear together are separated from each other. (Again, this is often done to create a particular rhythm or to stress a particular word.) Take, for example, Theseus's "But earthlier happy is the rose distilled / Than that which, withering on the virgin thorn, / Grows, lives, and dies in single blessedness" (1.1.78–80); here the phrase "withering on the virgin thorn" separates the pronoun ("which") from its verb ("grows"). Or take Lysander's lines that begin at 1.1.103: "My fortunes every way as fairly ranked / (If not with vantage) as Demetrius'," where the normal construction "as fairly ranked as Demetrius'" is interrupted by the insertion of the parenthetical "If not with vantage." In order to create for yourself sentences that seem more like the English of everyday speech, you may wish to rearrange the words, putting together the word clusters ("that which grows," "as fairly ranked as Demetrius'"). You will usually find that the sentence will gain in clarity but will lose its rhythm or shift its emphasis.

Locating and rearranging words that "belong together" is especially necessary in passages that separate basic sentence elements by long delaying or expanding interruptions. In some plays (*Hamlet*, for instance), long interrupted sentences are used to catch the audience up in the narrative or are used as a characterizing device. In *A Midsummer Night's Dream*, the interruptions are more often decorative lyrical passages. Hermia uses such an interrupted construction when she says to Lysander at 1.1.172–81:

> *I swear to thee* by Cupid's strongest bow,
> By his best arrow with the golden head,
> By the simplicity of Venus' doves,
> By that which knitteth souls and prospers loves,
> And by that fire which burned the Carthage queen
> When the false Trojan under sail was seen,
> By all the vows that ever men have broke
> (In number more than ever women spoke),
> In that same place thou hast appointed me,
> *Tomorrow* truly *will I meet with thee.*

Occasionally, rather than separating basic sentence elements, Shakespeare simply holds them back, delaying them until subordinate material has already been given. Lysander uses this kind of delaying structure when he says, at 1.1.134–36, "For aught that I could ever read, / Could ever hear by tale or history, / The course of true love never did run smooth" (where the basic sentence elements "The course of true love never did run smooth" are held back until two lines of explanatory material are introduced); Lysander's speech to Helena at 1.1.214–18 uses this same delayed construction:

> Tomorrow night when Phoebe doth behold
> Her silver visage in the wat'ry glass,
> Decking with liquid pearl the bladed grass
> (A time that lovers' flights doth still conceal),
> *Through Athens' gates have we devised to steal—*

delaying the basic sentence elements "we have devised

to steal through Athens' gates" and then doubly inverting them.

Finally, in *A Midsummer Night's Dream*, as in other of Shakespeare's plays, sentences are sometimes complicated not because of unusual structures or interruptions but because Shakespeare omits words and parts of words that English sentences normally require. (In conversation, we, too, often omit words. We say "Heard from him yet?" and our hearer supplies the missing "Have you.") Frequent reading of Shakespeare—and of other poets—trains us to supply such missing words. In plays written ten years or so after *A Midsummer Night's Dream*, Shakespeare uses omissions both of verbs and of nouns to great dramatic effect. In *A Midsummer Night's Dream* omissions are few and seem to result from the poet's wish to create regular iambic pentameter lines. At 1.1.76, for instance, Theseus says "Thrice-blessèd they that master so their blood" instead of "Thrice-blessèd *are* they." This omission creates a rhythmically regular line. At 1.1.166 ("Steal forth thy father's house tomorrow night"), the omission of the word *from* in the phrase "forth from" again creates a regular rhythm.

Shakespearean Wordplay

Shakespeare plays with language so often and so variously that entire books are written on the topic. His wordplay in *A Midsummer Night's Dream* is particularly interesting in the way it varies his usual use of puns and figurative language. A pun is a play on words that sound the same but that have different meanings. In *A Midsummer Night's Dream*, puns are found only occasionally, but, as with much of the language of this play, where they are used, they are used complexly. When, for example, Helena says (at 1.1.248–51),

> For, ere Demetrius looked on Hermia's eyne,
> He hailed down oaths that he was only mine;
> And when this hail some heat from Hermia felt,
> So he dissolved, and show'rs of oaths did melt—

the first use of the word *hail* means "to shower down, to pour," but, since it sounds exactly like the verb *hale*, it also carries the sense of "pull down," as if the oaths were being tugged down from the sky. The second use of the word *hail*, in the following line, is as a noun, and Demetrius's oaths are given the characteristics of hail: they feel heat, dissolve, and melt. This shift from *hail/ hale* as a verb to *hail* as a noun is an interestingly complex pun.

More often, in *A Midsummer Night's Dream*, we find instead a variation on Shakespeare's usual puns. In a complex variant on the pun, he has characters *confuse* words with other words that sound (more or less) the same but have very different meanings. (Such verbal confusions are now called "malapropisms.") Bottom is particularly inclined to this kind of speech. When he says, for example, "But I will *aggravate* my voice so that I will roar you as gently as any sucking dove" (1.2.78–80) he seems to be confusing *aggravate* with *moderate* or *mitigate* (soften, tone down). (In a different kind of confusion, his reference to the "sucking dove" mixes up the sucking [i.e., unweaned] lamb and the sitting [i.e., hatching] dove.) When he says "there we may rehearse most obscenely and courageously" (1.2.103–4), he is confusing *obscenely* with some other word (probably *seemly*) and confusing *courageously* either with a word that sounds a bit like it (perhaps *correctly*) or perhaps with the word *bravely*, which had the meaning both of "courageously" and of "splendidly, in a fine fashion."

Not only are puns and related wordplay used unusually and complexly in *A Midsummer Night's Dream*, but figurative language is also shifted away from Shakespeare's usual patterns. Instead of finding straightforward metaphors (i.e., plays on words in which one object or idea is expressed as if it were something else, something with which it shares common features), one is more likely to find extended similes, buried similes, and elaborate personifications. In a simile, one thing is said to be *like* or *as* another, as when Theseus charges that the moon "lingers my desires / Like to a stepdame or a dowager / Long withering out a young man's revenue" (1.1.4–6). Here the moon is compared to a stepmother or a widow with rights in her husband's property, and Theseus's desires are compared to the young man who has to wait to claim his inheritance. Many of the similes in this play begin as simple similes and then extend themselves into elaborate comparisons that take on some of the qualities of what we sometimes call "epic similes." In Lysander's words to Hermia at 1.1.136–51, for example, he first compares the briefness of love to a series of things thought of as transient: sounds, shadows, dreams. Then, with the comparison of love to "lightning in the collied [coal-black] night," the simile takes on a life of its own, as the lightning "unfolds both heaven and earth" and then is devoured by the darkness:

> The course of true love never did run smooth. . . .
> [Since,] if there were a sympathy in choice,
> War, death, or sickness did lay siege to it,
> Making it momentany as a sound,
> Swift as a shadow, short as any dream,
> Brief as the lightning in the collied night,
> That, in a spleen, unfolds both heaven and earth,
> And, ere a man hath power to say "Behold!"
> The jaws of darkness do devour it up.
> So quick bright things come to confusion.

(Note the powerful puns in the final line of this speech, where "So quick bright things" means, simultaneously, "So quickly do bright things" and "Thus quick [living, intense] bright things," and where *confusion* means both "destruction, ruin" and "disorder.")

One finds a much simpler example of an extended simile in Helena's charge to Hermia (1.1.186–88):

> Your eyes are lodestars and your tongue's sweet air
> More tunable than lark to shepherd's ear
> When wheat is green, when hawthorn buds appear—

where the third line elaborates the figure of the lark, to which Hermia's tongue has been compared.

Another kind of extended simile in this play is reminiscent of emblem books, where an idea is shown in the form of a picture under which is printed a name for the picture and an elaborate explanation. One finds the verbal equivalent of such an emblem in Helena's speech about Love (1.1.240–47). (Here the "picture" we are supposedly looking at is that of the boy Cupid, wearing a blindfold and bearing wings; Helena's words provide the standard "explanation" of the picture and its title, "Love"):

> Love looks not with the eyes but with the mind;
> And therefore is winged Cupid painted blind.
> Nor hath Love's mind of any judgment taste.
> Wings, and no eyes, figure unheedy haste.
> And therefore is Love said to be a child
> Because in choice he is so oft beguiled.
> As waggish boys in game themselves forswear,
> So the boy Love is perjured everywhere.

The entire speech could be transcribed as an extended

simile: "Love is like a boy who is winged and blind, because love is blind, without judgment, hasty, etc."

Often in *A Midsummer Night's Dream,* the simile, rather than being extended, is "buried" within the language. (Some readers might prefer to see these buried similes as metaphors.) For example, when Theseus says to Hermia (1.1.76–80):

> Thrice-blessèd they that master so their blood
> To undergo such maiden pilgrimage,
> But earthlier happy is the rose distilled
> Than that which, withering on the virgin thorn,
> Grows, lives, and dies in single blessedness—

under the surface of the language is a comparison of the unmarried woman to an unplucked rose and of the married woman to the rose that is plucked and its fragrance distilled into perfume. When Lysander says to Hermia (1.1.130–31): "How now, my love? Why is your cheek so pale? / How chance the roses there do fade so fast?" the buried simile likens red cheeks to roses. Hermia continues that simile when she responds (1.1.132–33): "Belike [probably] for want [lack] of rain, which I could well / Beteem [give] them from the tempest of my eyes," expanding the buried simile to include a comparison of weeping eyes to pouring rain. Hermia's "Keep word, Lysander. We must starve our sight / From lovers' food till morrow deep midnight" (1.1.227–28) includes a buried simile: the sight of the beloved is like food to the lover.

Finally, figurative language in *A Midsummer Night's Dream* often includes personification (i.e., abstract qualities are given human characteristics). To take a single example: when Theseus says to his master of the revels (1.1.14–16): "Awake the pert and nimble spirit of mirth.

/ Turn melancholy forth to funerals; / The pale companion is not for our pomp," he personifies both mirth and
melancholy, expanding the personification of melancholy by describing it as pale and using the condescend-
ing term *companion* (which here means "fellow").

Implied Stage Action

Finally, in reading Shakespeare's plays we should always
remember that what we are reading is a performance
script. The dialogue is written to be spoken by actors
who, at the same time, are moving, gesturing, picking up
objects, weeping, shaking their fists. Some stage action
is described in what are called "stage directions"; some
is suggested within the dialogue itself. Learn to be alert
to such signals as you stage the play in your imagination.
When, in *A Midsummer Night's Dream* at 2.1.60, Robin
Goodfellow says to the Fairy "room [i.e., stand aside],
fairy. Here comes Oberon," and the Fairy responds
"And here my mistress. Would that he were gone!" it is
almost certain that Robin and the Fairy would move
aside for the entrance of the king and queen of Fairyland. Similarly, a few lines later, when Titania orders
her fairies to "skip hence," it is almost certain that they
would obey her orders. Her later orders to them at line
149, "Fairies, away," show that, when they earlier "skip
hence," they do not leave the stage. At many places in *A
Midsummer Night's Dream*, signals to the reader are not
quite so clear. When Demetrius says to Helena at line
242 "Let me go," it is clear that she has earlier taken
hold of him, but it is not at all certain when she did so.
Nor is it certain when she turns him loose (or, perhaps,
when he pulls away from her) nor even when he exits.
(In our text, we have shown him leaving the stage two
lines before Helena's exit, but we could have placed his

exit several lines earlier, or have left him onstage until
Helena's exit.) In these uncertain situations, the director
and the actors and you, as reader, must decide what
makes for the most interesting, most likely, action.

Many scenes in this play give scope for imaginative
"staging": Just how do Oberon and Robin "anoint" the
eyes of their sleeping victims? How does Robin stage the
mock combat between Lysander and Demetrius? What
stage action accompanies the speeches of Titania to
(and about) the transformed Bottom: "Out of this wood
do not desire to go" (3.1.154); "Tie up my lover's tongue.
Bring him silently" (3.1.208); "So doth the woodbine
the sweet honeysuckle / Gently entwist; the female ivy
so / Enrings the barky fingers of the elm" (4.1.43–45)?

Learning to read the language of stage action repays
one many times over when one reaches scenes such as
the final scene of *A Midsummer Night's Dream*, where
much of the pleasure of the scene turns on our ability to
visualize the performance of "Pyramus and Thisbe"
before a scoffing court (as Wall provides a "chink"
through which the lovers whisper, as "Moon" defends
his bush and his lantern, as Thisbe imbrues her breast
with a "trusty sword").

It is immensely rewarding to work carefully with
Shakespeare's language so that the words, the sentences,
the wordplay, and the implied stage action all become
clear—as readers for the past four centuries have discovered. It may be more pleasurable to attend a good
performance of a play—though not everyone has
thought so. But the joy of being able to stage one of
Shakespeare's plays in one's imagination, to return to
passages that continue to yield further meanings (or
further questions) the more one reads them—these are
pleasures that, for many, rival (or at least augment)
those of the performed text, and certainly make it worth
considerable effort to "break the code" of Elizabethan

poetic drama and let free the remarkable language that makes up a Shakespeare text.

Shakespeare's Life

Surviving documents that give us glimpses into the life of William Shakespeare show us a playwright, poet, and actor who grew up in the market town of Stratford-upon-Avon, spent his professional life in London, and returned to Stratford a wealthy landowner. He was born in April 1564, died in April 1616, and is buried inside the chancel of Holy Trinity Church in Stratford.

We wish we could know more about the life of the world's greatest dramatist. His plays and poems are testaments to his wide reading—especially to his knowledge of Virgil, Ovid, Plutarch, Holinshed's *Chronicles*, and the Bible—and to his mastery of the English language, but we can only speculate about his education. We know that the King's New School in Stratford-upon-Avon was considered excellent. The school was one of the English "grammar schools" established to educate young men, primarily in Latin grammar and literature. As in other schools of the time, students began their studies at the age of four or five in the attached "petty school," and there learned to read and write in English, studying primarily the catechism from the Book of Common Prayer. After two years in the petty school, students entered the lower form (grade) of the grammar school, where they began the serious study of Latin grammar and Latin texts that would occupy most of the remainder of their school days. (Several Latin texts that Shakespeare used repeatedly in writing his plays and poems were texts that schoolboys memorized and recited.) Latin comedies were introduced early in the lower form; in the upper form, which the boys entered at age ten or eleven, students wrote their own Latin orations and declamations, studied Latin historians and rhetoricians, and began the study of Greek using the Greek New Testament.

Since the records of the Stratford "grammar school" do not survive, we cannot prove that William Shakespeare attended the school; however, every indication (his father's position as an alderman and bailiff of Stratford, the playwright's own knowledge of the Latin classics, scenes in the plays that recall grammar-school experiences—for example, *The Merry Wives of Windsor,* 4.1) suggests that he did. We also lack generally accepted documentation about Shakespeare's life after his schooling ended and his professional life in London began. His marriage in 1582 (at age eighteen) to Anne Hathaway and the subsequent births of his daughter Susanna (1583) and the twins Judith and Hamnet (1585) are recorded, but how he supported himself and where he lived are not known. Nor do we know when and why he left Stratford for the London theatrical world, nor how he rose to be the important figure in that world that he had become by the early 1590s.

We do know that by 1592 he had achieved some prominence in London as both an actor and a playwright. In that year was published a book by the playwright Robert Greene attacking an actor who had the audacity to write blank-verse drama and who was "in his own conceit [i.e., opinion] the only Shake-scene in a country." Since Greene's attack includes a parody of a line from one of Shakespeare's early plays, there is little doubt that it is Shakespeare to whom he refers, a "Shake-scene" who had aroused Greene's fury by successfully competing with university-educated dramatists like Greene himself. It was in 1593 that Shakespeare became a published poet. In that year he published his long narrative poem *Venus and Adonis;* in 1594, he followed it with *The Rape of Lucrece.* Both poems were dedicated to the young earl of Southampton (Henry Wriothesley), who may have become Shakespeare's patron.

It seems no coincidence that Shakespeare wrote these narrative poems at a time when the theaters were closed because of the plague, a contagious epidemic disease that devastated the population of London. When the theaters reopened in 1594, Shakespeare apparently resumed his double career of actor and playwright and began his long (and seemingly profitable) service as an acting-company shareholder. Records for December of 1594 show him to be a leading member of the Lord Chamberlain's Men. It was this company of actors, later named the King's Men, for whom he would be a principal actor, dramatist, and shareholder for the rest of his career.

So far as we can tell, that career spanned about twenty years. In the 1590s, he wrote his plays on English history as well as several comedies and at least two tragedies (*Titus Andronicus* and *Romeo and Juliet*). These histories, comedies, and tragedies are the plays credited to him in 1598 in a work, *Palladis Tamia,* that in one chapter compares English writers with "Greek, Latin, and Italian Poets." There the author, Francis Meres, claims that Shakespeare is comparable to the Latin dramatists Seneca for tragedy and Plautus for comedy, and calls him "the most excellent in both kinds for the stage." He also names him "mellifluous and honey-tongued Shakespeare": "I say," writes Meres, "that the Muses would speak with Shakespeare's fine filed phrase, if they would speak English." Since Meres also mentions Shakespeare's "sugared sonnets among his private friends," it is assumed that many of Shakespeare's sonnets (not published until 1609) were also written in the 1590s.

In 1599, Shakespeare's company built a theater for themselves across the river from London, naming it the Globe. The plays that are considered by many to be Shakespeare's major tragedies (*Hamlet, Othello, King Lear,* and *Macbeth*) were written while the company was resident in this theater, as were such comedies as *Twelfth Night* and *Measure for Measure.* Many of Shakespeare's plays were performed at court (both for Queen Elizabeth I and, after her death in 1603, for King James I), some were presented at the Inns of Court (the residences of London's legal societies), and some were doubtless performed in other towns, at the universities, and at great houses when the King's Men went on tour; otherwise, his plays from 1599 to 1608 were, so far as we know, performed only at the Globe. Between 1608 and 1612, Shakespeare wrote several plays—among them *The Winter's Tale* and *The Tempest*—presumably for the company's new indoor Blackfriars theater, though the plays seem to have been performed also at the Globe and at court. Surviving documents describe a performance of *The Winter's Tale* in 1611 at the Globe, for example, and performances of *The Tempest* in 1611 and 1613 at the royal palace of Whitehall.

Shakespeare wrote very little after 1612, the year in which he probably wrote *King Henry VIII.* (It was at a performance of *Henry VIII* in 1613 that the Globe caught fire and burned to the ground.) Sometime between 1610 and 1613 he seems to have returned to live in Stratford-upon-Avon, where he owned a large house and considerable property, and where his wife and his two daughters and their husbands lived. (His son, Hamnet, had died in 1596.) During his professional years in London, Shakespeare had presumably derived income from the acting company's profits as well as from his own career as an actor, from the sale of his play manuscripts to the acting company, and, after 1599, from his shares as an owner of the Globe. It was presumably that income, carefully invested in land and other property, that made him the wealthy man that surviving documents show him to have become. It is also assumed that William Shakespeare's growing wealth and reputation played some part in inclining the crown, in 1596, to grant John Shakespeare, William's father, the coat of arms that he had so long sought. William Shakespeare died in Stratford on April 23, 1616 (according to the epitaph carved under his bust in Holy Trinity Church) and was buried on April 25. Seven years after his death, his collected plays were published as *Mr. William Shakespeares Comedies, Histories, & Tragedies* (the work now known as the First Folio).

The years in which Shakespeare wrote were among the most exciting in English history. Intellectually, the discovery, translation, and printing of Greek and Roman classics were making available a set of works and worldviews that interacted complexly with Christian texts and beliefs. The result was a questioning, a vital intellectual ferment, that provided energy for the period's amazing dramatic and literary output and that fed directly into Shakespeare's plays. The Ghost in *Hamlet,* for example, is wonderfully complicated in part because he is a figure from Roman tragedy—the spirit of the dead returning to seek revenge—who at the same time inhabits a Christian hell (or purgatory); Hamlet's description of humankind reflects at one moment the Neoplatonic wonderment at mankind ("What a piece of work is a man!") and, at the next, the Christian disparagement of human sinners ("And yet, to me, what is this quintessence of dust?").

As intellectual horizons expanded, so also did geographical and cosmological horizons. New worlds—

both North and South America—were explored, and in them were found human beings who lived and worshiped in ways radically different from those of Renaissance Europeans and Englishmen. The universe during these years also seemed to shift and expand. Copernicus had earlier theorized that the earth was not the center of the cosmos but revolved as a planet around the sun. Galileo's telescope, created in 1609, allowed scientists to see that Copernicus had been correct: the universe was not organized with the earth at the center, nor was it so nicely circumscribed as people had, until that time, thought. In terms of expanding horizons, the impact of these discoveries on people's beliefs—religious, scientific, and philosophical—cannot be overstated.

London, too, rapidly expanded and changed during the years (from the early 1590s to around 1610) that Shakespeare lived there. London—the center of England's government, its economy, its royal court, its overseas trade—was, during these years, becoming an exciting metropolis, drawing to it thousands of new citizens every year. Troubled by overcrowding, by poverty, by recurring epidemics of the plague, London was also a mecca for the wealthy and the aristocratic, and for those who sought advancement at court, or power in government or finance or trade. One hears in Shakespeare's plays the voices of London—the struggles for power, the fear of venereal disease, the language of buying and selling. One hears as well the voices of Stratford-upon-Avon—references to the nearby Forest of Arden, to sheep herding, to small-town gossip, to village fairs and markets. Part of the richness of Shakespeare's work is the influence felt there of the various worlds in which he lived: the world of metropolitan London, the world of small-town and rural England, the world of the theater, and the worlds of craftsmen and shepherds.

That Shakespeare inhabited such worlds we know from surviving London and Stratford documents, as well as from the evidence of the plays and poems themselves. From such records we can sketch the dramatist's life. We know from his works that he was a voracious reader. We know from legal and business documents that he was a multifaceted theater man who became a wealthy landowner. We know a bit about his family life and a fair amount about his legal and financial dealings. Most scholars today depend upon such evidence as they draw their picture of the world's greatest playwright. Such, however, has not always been the case. Until the late eighteenth century, the William Shakespeare who lived in most biographies was the creation of legend and tradition. This was the Shakespeare who was supposedly caught poaching deer at Charlecote, the estate of Sir Thomas Lucy close by Stratford; this was the Shakespeare who fled from Sir Thomas's vengeance and made his way in London by taking care of horses outside a playhouse; this was the Shakespeare who reportedly could barely read, but whose natural gifts were extraordinary, whose father was a butcher who allowed his gifted son sometimes to help in the butcher shop, where William supposedly killed calves "in a high style," making a speech for the occasion. It was this legendary William Shakespeare whose Falstaff (in *1* and *2 Henry IV*) so pleased Queen Elizabeth that she demanded a play about Falstaff in love, and demanded that it be written in fourteen days (hence the existence of *The Merry Wives of Windsor*). It was this legendary Shakespeare who reached the top of his acting career in the roles of the Ghost in *Hamlet* and old Adam in *As You Like It*—and who died of a fever contracted by drinking too hard at "a merry meeting" with the poets Michael Drayton and Ben Jonson. This legendary Shakespeare is a rambunctious, undisciplined man, as attractively "wild" as his plays were seen by earlier generations to be. Unfortunately, there is no trace of evidence to support these wonderful stories.

Perhaps in response to the disreputable Shakespeare of legend—or perhaps in response to the fragmentary and, for some, all-too-ordinary Shakespeare documented by surviving records—some people since the mid-nineteenth century have argued that William Shakespeare could not have written the plays that bear his name. These persons have put forward some dozen names as more likely authors, among them Queen Elizabeth, Sir Francis Bacon, Edward de Vere (earl of Oxford), and Christopher Marlowe. Such attempts to find what for these people is a more believable author of the plays is a tribute to the regard in which the plays are held. Unfortunately for their claims, the documents that exist that provide evidence for the facts of Shakespeare's life tie him inextricably to the body of plays and poems that bear his name. Unlikely as it seems to those who want the works to have been written by an aristocrat, a university graduate, or an "important" person, the plays and poems seem clearly to have been produced by a man from Stratford-upon-Avon with a very good "grammar-school" education and a life of experience in London and in the world of the London theater. How this particular man produced the works that dominate the cultures of much of the world almost four hundred years after his death is one of life's mysteries—and one that will continue to tease our imaginations as we continue to delight in his plays and poems.

Shakespeare's Theater

The actors of Shakespeare's time are known to have performed plays in a great variety of locations. They played at court (that is, in the great halls of such royal residences as Whitehall, Hampton Court, and Greenwich); they played in halls at the universities of Oxford and Cambridge, and at the Inns of Court (the residences in London of the legal societies); and they also played in the private houses of great lords and civic officials. Sometimes acting companies went on tour from London into the provinces, often (but not only) when outbreaks of bubonic plague in the capital forced the closing of theaters to reduce the possibility of contagion in crowded audiences. In the provinces the actors usually staged their plays in churches (until around 1600) or in guildhalls. While surviving records show only a handful of occasions when actors played at inns while on tour, London inns were important playing places up until the 1590s.

The building of theaters in London had begun only shortly before Shakespeare wrote his first plays in the 1590s. These theaters were of two kinds: outdoor or public playhouses that could accommodate large numbers of playgoers, and indoor or private theaters for much smaller audiences. What is usually regarded as the first London outdoor public playhouse was called simply the Theatre. James Burbage—the father of Richard Burbage, who was perhaps the most famous actor in Shakespeare's company—built it in 1576 in an area north of the city of London called Shoreditch. Among the more famous of the other public playhouses that capitalized on the new fashion were the Curtain and the Fortune (both also built north of the city), the Rose, the Swan, the Globe, and the Hope (all located on the Bankside, a region just across the Thames south of the city of London). All these playhouses had to be built outside the jurisdiction of the city of London because many civic officials were hostile to the performance of drama and repeatedly petitioned the royal council to abolish it.

The theaters erected on the Bankside (a region under the authority of the Church of England, whose head was the monarch) shared the neighborhood with houses of prostitution and with the Paris Garden, where the blood sports of bearbaiting and bullbaiting were carried on. There may have been no clear distinction between playhouses and buildings for such sports, for we know that the Hope was used for both plays and baiting and that Philip Henslowe, owner of the Rose and, later, partner in the ownership of the Fortune, was also a partner in a monopoly on baiting. All these forms of entertainment were easily accessible to Londoners by boat across the Thames or over London Bridge.

Evidently Shakespeare's company prospered on the Bankside. They moved there in 1599. Threatened by difficulties in renewing the lease on the land where their first theater (the Theatre) had been built, Shakespeare's company took advantage of the Christmas holiday in 1598 to dismantle the Theatre and transport its timbers across the Thames to the Bankside, where, in 1599, these timbers were used in the building of the Globe. The weather in late December 1598 is recorded as having been especially harsh. It was so cold that the Thames was "nigh [nearly] frozen," and there was heavy snow. Perhaps the weather aided Shakespeare's company in eluding their landlord, the snow hiding their activity and the freezing of the Thames allowing them to slide the timbers across to the Bankside without paying tolls for repeated trips over London Bridge. Attractive as this narrative is, it remains just as likely that the heavy snow hampered transport of the timbers in wagons through the London streets to the river. It also must be remembered that the Thames was, according to report, only "nigh frozen" and therefore as impassable as it ever was. Whatever the precise circumstances of this fascinating event in English theater history, Shakespeare's company was able to begin playing at their new Globe theater on the Bankside in 1599. After the first Globe burned down in 1613 during the staging of Shakespeare's *Henry VIII* (its thatch roof was set alight by cannon fire called for by the performance), Shakespeare's company immediately rebuilt on the same location. The second Globe seems to have been a grander structure than its predecessor. It remained in use until the beginning of the English Civil War in 1642, when Parliament officially closed the theaters. Soon thereafter it was pulled down.

The public theaters of Shakespeare's time were very different buildings from our theaters today. First of all, they were open-air playhouses. As recent excavations of the Rose and the Globe confirm, some were polygonal or roughly circular in shape; the Fortune, however, was square. The most recent estimates of their size put the diameter of these buildings at 72 feet (the Rose) to 100 feet (the Globe), but we know that they held vast audiences of two or three thousand, who must have been squeezed together quite tightly. Some of these spectators paid extra to sit or stand in the two or three levels of roofed galleries that extended, on the upper levels, all the way around the theater and surrounded an open space. In this space were the stage and, perhaps, the tiring house (what we would call dressing rooms), as well as the so-called yard. In the yard stood the spectators who chose to pay less, the ones whom Hamlet contemptuously called "groundlings." For a roof they had only the sky, and so they were exposed to all kinds of weather. They stood on a floor that was sometimes made of mortar and sometimes of ash mixed with the shells of hazelnuts. The latter provided a porous and therefore dry footing for the crowd, and the shells may have been more comfortable to stand on because they were not as hard as mortar. Availability of shells may not have been a problem if hazelnuts were a favorite food for Shakespeare's audiences to munch on as they watched his plays. Archaeologists who are today unearthing the remains of theaters from this period have discovered quantities of these nutshells on theater sites.

Unlike the yard, the stage itself was covered by a roof. Its ceiling, called "the heavens," is thought to have been elaborately painted to depict the sun, moon, stars, and planets. Just how big the stage was remains hard to determine. We have a single sketch of part of the interior of the Swan. A Dutchman named Johannes de Witt visited this theater around 1596 and sent a sketch of it back to his friend, Arend van Buchel. Because van Buchel found de Witt's letter and sketch of interest, he copied both into a book. It is van Buchel's copy, adapted, it seems, to the shape and size of the page in his book, that survives. In this sketch, the stage appears to be a large rectangular platform that thrusts far out into the yard, perhaps even as far as the center of the circle formed by the surrounding galleries. This drawing, combined with the specifications for the size of the stage in the building contract for the Fortune, has led scholars to conjecture that the stage on which Shakespeare's plays were performed must have measured approximately 43 feet in width and 27 feet in depth, a vast acting area. But the digging up of a large part of the Rose by archaeologists has provided evidence of a quite different stage design. The Rose stage was a platform tapered at the corners and much shallower than what seems to be depicted in the van Buchel sketch. Indeed, its measurements seem to be about 37.5 feet across at its widest point and only 15.5 feet deep. Because the surviving indications of stage size and design differ from each other so much, it is possible that the stages in other theaters, like the Theatre, the Curtain, and the Globe (the outdoor playhouses where we know that Shakespeare's plays were performed), were different from those at both the Swan and the Rose.

After about 1608 Shakespeare's plays were staged not only at the Globe but also at an indoor or private playhouse in Blackfriars. This theater had been constructed in 1596 by James Burbage in an upper hall of a former Dominican priory or monastic house. Although Henry VIII had dissolved all English monasteries in the 1530s (shortly after he had founded the Church of England), the area remained under church, rather than hostile civic, control. The hall that Burbage had purchased and renovated was a large one in which Parliament had once met. In the private theater that he constructed, the stage, lit by candles, was built across the narrow end of the hall, with boxes flanking it. The rest of the hall offered seating room only. Because there was no provision for standing room, the largest audience it could hold was less than a thousand, or about a quarter of what the Globe could accommodate. Admission to Blackfriars was correspondingly more expensive. Instead of a penny to stand in the yard at the Globe, it cost a minimum of sixpence to get into Blackfriars. The best seats at the Globe (in the Lords' Room in the gallery above and behind the stage) cost sixpence; but the boxes flanking the stage at Blackfriars were half a crown, or five times sixpence. Some spectators who were particularly interested in displaying themselves paid even more to sit on stools on the Blackfriars stage.

Whether in the outdoor or indoor playhouses, the

stages of Shakespeare's time were different from ours. They were not separated from the audience by the dropping of a curtain between acts and scenes. Therefore the playwrights of the time had to find other ways of signaling to the audience that one scene (to be imagined as occurring in one location at a given time) had ended and the next (to be imagined at perhaps a different location at a later time) had begun. The customary way used by Shakespeare and many of his contemporaries was to have everyone on stage exit at the end of one scene and have one or more different characters enter to begin the next. In a few cases, where characters remain onstage from one scene to another, the dialogue or stage action makes the change of location clear, and the characters are generally to be imagined as having moved from one place to another. For example, in *Romeo and Juliet,* Romeo and his friends remain onstage in Act 1 from scene 4 to scene 5, but they are represented as having moved between scenes from the street that leads to Capulet's house into Capulet's house itself. The new location is signaled in part by the appearance onstage of Capulet's servingmen carrying napkins, something they would not take into the streets. Playwrights had to be quite resourceful in the use of hand properties, like the napkin, or in the use of dialogue to specify where the action was taking place in their plays because, in contrast to most of today's theaters, the playhouses of Shakespeare's time did not use movable scenery to dress the stage and make the setting precise. As another consequence of this difference, however, the playwrights of Shakespeare's time did not have to specify exactly where the action of their plays was set when they did not choose to do so, and much of the action of their plays is tied to no specific place.

Usually Shakespeare's stage is referred to as a "bare stage," to distinguish it from the stages of the last two or three centuries with their elaborate sets. But the stage in Shakespeare's time was not completely bare. Philip Henslowe, owner of the Rose, lists in his inventory of stage properties a rock, three tombs, and two mossy banks. Stage directions in plays of the time also call for such things as thrones (or "states"), banquets (presumably tables with plaster replicas of food on them), and beds and tombs to be pushed onto the stage. Thus the stage often held more than the actors.

The actors did not limit their performing to the stage alone. Occasionally they went beneath the stage, as the Ghost appears to do in the first act of *Hamlet*. From there they could emerge onto the stage through a trapdoor. They could retire behind the hangings across the back of the stage (or the front of the tiring house), as, for example, the actor playing Polonius does when he hides behind the arras. Sometimes the hangings could be drawn back during a performance to "discover" one or more actors behind them. When performance required that an actor appear "above," as when Juliet is imagined to stand at the window of her chamber in the famous and misnamed "balcony scene," then the actor probably climbed the stairs to the gallery over the back of the stage and temporarily shared it with some of the spectators. The stage was also provided with ropes and winches so that actors could descend from, and reascend to, the "heavens."

Perhaps the greatest difference between dramatic performances in Shakespeare's time and ours was that in Shakespeare's England the roles of women were played by boys. (Some of these boys grew up to take male roles in their maturity.) There were no women in the acting companies, only in the audience. It had not always been so in the history of the English stage. There are records of women on English stages in the thirteenth and fourteenth centuries, two hundred years before

Shakespeare's plays were performed. After the accession of James I in 1603, the queen of England and her ladies took part in entertainments at court called masques, and with the reopening of the theaters in 1660 at the restoration of Charles II, women again took their place on the public stage.

The chief competitors for the companies of adult actors such as the one to which Shakespeare belonged and for which he wrote were companies of exclusively boy actors. The competition was most intense in the early 1600s. There were then two principal children's companies: the Children of Paul's (the choirboys from St. Paul's Cathedral, whose private playhouse was near the cathedral); and the Children of the Chapel Royal (the choirboys from the monarch's private chapel, who performed at the Blackfriars theater built by Burbage in 1596, which Shakespeare's company had been stopped from using by local residents who objected to crowds). In *Hamlet* Shakespeare writes of "an aerie [nest] of children, little eyases [hawks], that cry out on the top of question and are most tyrannically clapped for 't. These are now the fashion and . . . berattle the common stages [attack the public theaters]." In the long run, the adult actors prevailed. The Children of Paul's dissolved around 1606. By about 1608 the Children of the Chapel Royal had been forced to stop playing at the Blackfriars theater, which was then taken over by the King's Men, Shakespeare's own troupe.

Acting companies and theaters of Shakespeare's time were organized in different ways. For example, Philip Henslowe owned the Rose and leased it to companies of actors, who paid him from their takings. Henslowe would act as manager of these companies, initially paying playwrights for their plays and buying properties, recovering his outlay from the actors. Shakespeare's company, however, managed itself, with the principal actors, Shakespeare among them, having the status of "sharers" and the right to a share in the takings, as well as the responsibility for a part of the expenses. Five of the sharers themselves, Shakespeare among them, owned the Globe. As actor, as sharer in an acting company and in ownership of theaters, and as playwright, Shakespeare was about as involved in the theatrical industry as one could imagine. Although Shakespeare and his fellows prospered, their status under the law was conditional upon the protection of powerful patrons. "Common players"—those who did not have patrons or masters—were classed in the language of the law with "vagabonds and sturdy beggars." So the actors had to secure for themselves the official rank of servants of patrons. Among the patrons under whose protection Shakespeare's company worked were the lord chamberlain and, after the accession of King James in 1603, the king himself.

We are now perhaps on the verge of learning a great deal more about the theaters in which Shakespeare and his contemporaries performed—or at least of opening up new questions about them. Already about 70 percent of the Rose has been excavated, as has about 10 percent of the second Globe, the one built in 1614. It is to be hoped that soon more will be available for study. These are exciting times for students of Shakespeare's stage.

The Publication of Shakespeare's Plays

Eighteen of Shakespeare's plays found their way into print during the playwright's lifetime, but there is nothing to suggest that he took any interest in their publication. These eighteen appeared separately in editions called quartos. Their pages were not much larger than the one you are now reading, and these little books were sold unbound for a few pence. The earliest of the quartos that still survive were printed in 1594, the year that both *Titus Andronicus* and a version of the play now called *2 King Henry VI* became available. While almost every one of these early quartos displays on its title page the name of the acting company that performed the play, only about half provide the name of the playwright, Shakespeare. The first quarto edition to bear the name Shakespeare on its title page is *Love's Labor's Lost* of 1598. A few of these quartos were popular with the book-buying public of Shakespeare's lifetime; for example, quarto *Richard II* went through five editions between 1597 and 1615. But most of the quartos were far from best-sellers; *Love's Labor's Lost* (1598), for instance, was not reprinted in quarto until 1631. After Shakespeare's death, two more of his plays appeared in quarto format: *Othello* in 1622 and *The Two Noble Kinsmen*, coauthored with John Fletcher, in 1634.

In 1623, seven years after Shakespeare's death, *Mr. William Shakespeares Comedies, Histories, & Tragedies* was published. This printing offered readers in a single book thirty-six of the thirty-eight plays now thought to have been written by Shakespeare, including eighteen that had never been printed before. And it offered them in a style that was then reserved for serious literature and scholarship. The plays were arranged in double columns on pages nearly a foot high. This large page size is called "folio," as opposed to the smaller "quarto," and the 1623 volume is usually called the Shakespeare First Folio. It is reputed to have sold for the lordly price of a pound. (One copy at the Folger Library is marked fifteen shillings—that is, three-quarters of a pound.)

In a preface to the First Folio entitled "To the great Variety of Readers," two of Shakespeare's former fellow actors in the King's Men, John Heminge and Henry

Condell, wrote that they themselves had collected their dead companion's plays. They suggested that they had seen his own papers: "we have scarce received from him a blot in his papers." The title page of the Folio declared that the plays within it had been printed "according to the True Original Copies." Comparing the Folio to the quartos, Heminge and Condell disparaged the quartos, advising their readers that "before you were abused with divers stolen and surreptitious copies, maimed, and deformed by the frauds and stealths of injurious impostors." Many Shakespeareans of the eighteenth and nineteenth centuries believed Heminge and Condell and regarded the Folio plays as superior to anything in the quartos.

Once we begin to examine the Folio plays in detail, it becomes less easy to take at face value the word of Heminge and Condell about the superiority of the Folio texts. For example, of the first nine plays in the Folio (one quarter of the entire collection), four were essentially reprinted from earlier quarto printings that Heminge and Condell had disparaged; and four have now been identified as printed from copies written in the hand of a professional scribe of the 1620s named Ralph Crane; the ninth, *The Comedy of Errors,* was apparently also printed from a manuscript, but one whose origin cannot be readily identified. Evidently then, eight of the first nine plays in the First Folio were not printed, in spite of what the Folio title page announces, "according to the True Original Copies," or Shakespeare's own papers, and the source of the ninth is unknown. Since today's editors have been forced to treat Heminge and Condell's pronouncements with skepticism, they must choose whether to base their own editions upon quartos or the Folio on grounds other than Heminge and Condell's story of where the quarto and Folio versions originated.

Editors have often fashioned their own narratives to explain what lies behind the quartos and Folio. They have said that Heminge and Condell meant to criticize only a few of the early quartos, the ones that offer much shorter and sometimes quite different, often garbled, versions of plays. Among the examples of these are the 1600 quarto of *Henry V* (the Folio offers a much fuller version) or the 1603 *Hamlet* quarto (in 1604 a different, much longer form of the play got into print as a quarto). Early in this century editors speculated that these questionable texts were produced when someone in the audience took notes from the plays' dialogue during performances and then employed "hack poets" to fill out the notes. The poor results were then sold to a publisher and presented in print as Shakespeare's plays. More recently this story has given way to another in which the shorter versions are said to be recreations from memory of Shakespeare's plays by actors who wanted to stage them in the provinces but lacked manuscript copies. Most of the quartos offer much better texts than these so-called bad quartos. Indeed, in most of the quartos we find texts that are at least equal to or better than what is printed in the Folio. Many of this century's Shakespeare enthusiasts have persuaded themselves that most of the quartos were set into type directly from Shakespeare's own papers, although there is nothing on which to base this conclusion except the desire for it to be true. Thus speculation continues about how the Shakespeare plays got to be printed. All that we have are the printed texts.

The book collector who was most successful in bringing together copies of the quartos and the First Folio was Henry Clay Folger, founder of the Folger Shakespeare Library in Washington, D.C. While it is estimated that there survive around the world only about 230 copies of the First Folio, Mr. Folger was able to acquire more than seventy-five copies, as well as a large number of fragments, for the library that bears his name. He also amassed a substantial number of quartos. For example, only fourteen copies of the First Quarto of *Love's Labor's Lost* are known to exist, and three are at the Folger Shakespeare Library. As a consequence of Mr. Folger's labors, twentieth-century scholars visiting the Folger Library have been able to learn a great deal about sixteenth- and seventeenth-century printing and, particularly, about the printing of Shakespeare's plays. And Mr. Folger did not stop at the First Folio, but collected many copies of later editions of Shakespeare, beginning with the Second Folio (1632), the Third (1663–64), and the Fourth (1685). Each of these later folios was based on its immediate predecessor and was edited anonymously. The first editor of Shakespeare whose name we know was Nicholas Rowe, whose first edition came out in 1709. Mr. Folger collected this edition and many, many more by Rowe's successors.

An Introduction to This Text

A Midsummer Night's Dream was first printed in 1600 as a quarto. Then in 1619 someone slightly edited a copy of the 1600 quarto, adding a few stage directions and, perhaps, supplying some obvious verbal corrections, to make it the basis of a second quarto edition of the play. A copy of this 1619 quarto was, in turn, annotated and used as printer's copy for the First Folio text published in 1623. Again both stage directions and a few words of dialogue were affected. Chief among the changes introduced into the Folio text was the substitution of Egeus for Philostrate in Act 5, scene 1. Some scholars think that whoever annotated the 1619 text before it was reprinted in the Folio must have referred to a manuscript of the play that had actually been used in the theater, but this conjecture rests on the most slender evidence.

The present edition is based directly on the earliest quarto of 1600.* For the convenience of the reader, we have modernized the punctuation and the spelling of the quarto. Sometimes we go so far as to modernize certain old forms of words; for example, when *a* means "he," we change it to *he;* we change *mo* to *more* and *ye* to *you.* But it has not been our editorial practice in any of the plays to modernize some words that sound distinctly different from modern forms. For example, when the early printed texts read *sith* or *apricocks* or *porpentine,* we have not modernized to *since, apricots, porcupine.* When the forms *an, and,* or *and if* appear instead of the modern form *if,* we have reduced *and* to *an* but have not changed any of these forms to their modern equivalent, *if.* We also modernize and, where necessary, correct passages in foreign languages, unless an error in the early printed text can be reasonably explained as a joke.

Whenever we change the wording of the First Quarto or add anything to its stage directions, we mark the change by enclosing it in superior half-brackets (⌐ ⌐). We want our readers to be immediately aware when we have intervened. (Only when we correct an obvious typographical error in the First Quarto does the change not get marked.) Whenever we change the First Quarto's wording or change its punctuation so that meaning changes, we list the change in the textual notes at the

*We have also consulted the computerized text of the First Quarto provided by the Text Archive of the Oxford University Computing Centre, to which we are grateful.

back of the book, even if all we have done is fix an obvious error.

We, like a great many editors before us, regularize a number of the proper names. For example, more often than not, the character Robin Goodfellow enters and speaks (according to the stage directions and speech prefixes) under this, his proper name. Sometimes, however, he appears under the name "Puck." He is, as he himself tells us, a puck or a hobgoblin. Most editors since Nicholas Rowe in 1709 have used the name "Puck" for Robin throughout their editions, but we choose, instead, to employ the proper name "Robin Goodfellow" throughout this edition. Sometimes Nick Bottom, the weaver, is referred to as "Clown" in stage directions and speech prefixes; again we use his proper name throughout. Finally, the workers who rehearse and stage a play for Theseus and Hippolyta are often designated in the speech prefixes by the names of their roles rather than by their proper names; e.g., Bottom speaks as "Pyramus," his role. In our speech prefixes we supply both the name of the character and the name of his role. We expand the often severely abbreviated forms of names used as speech headings in early printed texts into the full names of the characters. Variations in the speech headings of the early printed texts are recorded in the textual notes.

This edition differs from many earlier ones in its efforts to aid the reader in imagining the play as a performance rather than as a series of fictional events. Thus stage directions are written with reference to the stage. For example, in Act 3, scene 1, when the workers are rehearsing their play, they want to know if the moon will shine the night that they hope to perform it. In the fiction of the play, they consult an almanac to find out, and some editors print a stage direction of the form *"Quince consults an almanac."* However, in staging the play, no actor need use an almanac itself; any book of

reasonable size will do as a hand prop. And so, writing
stage directions from the perspective of the stage, we
print *"Quince takes out a book."* Whenever it is reasonably certain, in our view, that a speech is accompanied
by a particular action, we provide a stage direction
describing the action. (Occasional exceptions to this
rule occur when the action is so obvious that to add a
stage direction would insult the reader.) Stage directions for the entrance of characters in mid-scene are,
with rare exceptions, placed so that they immediately
precede the characters' participation in the scene, even
though these entrances may appear somewhat earlier in
the early printed texts. Whenever we move a stage
direction, we record this change in the textual notes.
Latin stage directions (e.g., *Exeunt*) are translated into
English (e.g., *They exit*).

In the present edition, as well, we mark with a dash
any change of address within a speech, unless a stage
direction intervenes. When the *-ed* ending of a word is to
be pronounced, we mark it with an accent.

Like editors for the past two centuries, we print
metrically linked lines in the following way:

HERMIA
    So is Lysander.
THESEUS   In himself he is.

However, when there are a number of short verse-lines
that can be linked in more than one way, we do not, with
rare exceptions, indent any of them.

The Explanatory Notes

The notes that appear on the pages facing the text are
designed to provide readers with the help that they may
need to enjoy the play. Whenever the meaning of a word

in the text is not readily accessible in a good contemporary dictionary, we offer the meaning in a note. Sometimes we provide a note even when the relevant meaning is to be found in the dictionary but when the word has acquired since Shakespeare's time other potentially confusing meanings. In our notes, we try to offer modern synonyms for Shakespeare's words. We also try to indicate to the reader the connection between the word in the play and the modern synonym. For example, Shakespeare sometimes uses the word *head* to mean "source," but, for modern readers, there may be no connection evident between these two words. We provide the connection by explaining Shakespeare's usage as follows: "**head:** fountainhead, source." On some occasions, a whole phrase or clause needs explanation. Then we rephrase in our own words the difficult passage, and add at the end synonyms for individual words in the passage. When scholars have been unable to determine the meaning of a word or phrase, we acknowledge the uncertainty.

A MIDSUMMER
NIGHT'S DREAM

Characters in the Play

HERMIA ⎫
LYSANDER ⎬ *four lovers*
HELENA ⎪
DEMETRIUS ⎭

THESEUS, duke of Athens
HIPPOLYTA, queen of the Amazons
EGEUS, father to Hermia
PHILOSTRATE, master of the revels to Theseus

NICK BOTTOM, weaver
PETER QUINCE, carpenter
FRANCIS FLUTE, bellows-mender
TOM SNOUT, tinker
SNUG, joiner
ROBIN STARVELING, tailor

OBERON, king of the Fairies
TITANIA, queen of the Fairies
ROBIN GOODFELLOW, a "puck," or hobgoblin, in Ober-
    on's service
A FAIRY, in the service of Titania
PEASEBLOSSOM ⎫
COBWEB ⎬ *fairies attending upon Titania*
MOTE ⎪
MUSTARDSEED ⎭

Lords and Attendants on Theseus and Hippolyta
Other Fairies in the trains of Titania and Oberon

3

A
MIDSUMMER
NIGHT'S DREAM

ACT 1

1.1   Theseus, duke of Athens, is planning the festivities for his upcoming wedding to the newly captured Amazon, Hippolyta. Egeus arrives with his daughter Hermia and her two suitors, Lysander (the man she wants to marry) and Demetrius (the man her father wants her to marry). Egeus demands that Theseus enforce Athenian law upon Hermia and execute her if she refuses to marry Demetrius. Theseus threatens Hermia with either lifelong chastity or death if she continues to disobey her father. Lysander and Hermia make plans to flee Athens. They reveal their plan to Helena, Hermia's friend, who is in love with Demetrius. To win Demetrius's favor, Helena decides to tell him about Lysander and Hermia's planned elopement.

---

1. **our nuptial hour:** the time for our wedding
4. **lingers:** delays, prolongs
5–6. **Like . . . revenue:** i.e., in the same way that a stepmother or a widow with rights in her dead husband's property (1) makes a young heir wait to inherit it, or (2) wastes it, or (3) has a claim on the young man's income until she dies
7. **steep themselves:** i.e., be absorbed (literally, soak themselves)
11. **solemnities:** festive ceremonies
14. **pert:** lively
16. **pale companion:** i.e., melancholy (**Companion** is a term of contempt, meaning "fellow.")
17–18. **I wooed . . . injuries:** In stories about Theseus, he overcomes Hippolyta in battle with the Amazons and then marries her.
20. **triumph:** public festivity

⌜ACT 1⌝

⌜Scene 1⌝

Enter Theseus, Hippolyta, ⌜and Philostrate,⌝ with others.

THESEUS
Now, fair Hippolyta, our nuptial hour
Draws on apace. Four happy days bring in
Another moon. But, O, methinks how slow
This old moon ⌜wanes!⌝ She lingers my desires
Like to a stepdame or a dowager   5
Long withering out a young man's revenue.

HIPPOLYTA
Four days will quickly steep themselves in night;
Four nights will quickly dream away the time;
And then the moon, like to a silver bow
⌜New⌝-bent in heaven, shall behold the night   10
Of our solemnities.

THESEUS   Go, Philostrate,
Stir up the Athenian youth to merriments.
Awake the pert and nimble spirit of mirth.
Turn melancholy forth to funerals;   15
The pale companion is not for our pomp.
                                        ⌜*Philostrate exits.*⌝
Hippolyta, I wooed thee with my sword
And won thy love doing thee injuries,
But I will wed thee in another key,
With pomp, with triumph, and with reveling.   20

7

32. **feigning voice:** a voice singing softly; **feigning love:** pretended love

33. **the impression of her fantasy:** i.e., her imagination, on which you have impressed your image

34. **gauds:** (1) playthings; (2) showy things; **conceits:** fancy trinkets

35. **Knacks:** knickknacks

36. **prevailment:** influence

40. **Be it so:** i.e., if

44. **this gentleman:** Demetrius

46. **Immediately:** directly, i.e., with nothing intervening between sentence and actual punishment

47. **Be advised:** i.e., think carefully

*Enter Egeus and his daughter Hermia, and Lysander
and Demetrius.*

EGEUS
Happy be Theseus, our renownèd duke!
THESEUS
Thanks, good Egeus. What's the news with thee?
EGEUS
Full of vexation come I, with complaint
Against my child, my daughter Hermia.—
Stand forth, Demetrius.—My noble lord,   25
This man hath my consent to marry her.—
Stand forth, Lysander.—And, my gracious duke,
This man hath bewitched the bosom of my child.—
Thou, thou, Lysander, thou hast given her rhymes
And interchanged love tokens with my child.   30
Thou hast by moonlight at her window sung
With feigning voice verses of feigning love
And stol'n the impression of her fantasy
With bracelets of thy hair, rings, gauds, conceits,
Knacks, trifles, nosegays, sweetmeats—messengers   35
Of strong prevailment in unhardened youth.
With cunning hast thou filched my daughter's heart,
Turned her obedience (which is due to me)
To stubborn harshness.—And, my gracious duke,
Be it so she will not here before your Grace   40
Consent to marry with Demetrius,
I beg the ancient privilege of Athens:
As she is mine, I may dispose of her,
Which shall be either to this gentleman
Or to her death, according to our law   45
Immediately provided in that case.
THESEUS
What say you, Hermia? Be advised, fair maid.
To you, your father should be as a god,
One that composed your beauties, yea, and one

52. **leave:** i.e., leave undisturbed; or, perhaps, abandon

56. **in this kind:** in this case; **wanting . . . voice:** lacking your father's support

62. **concern my modesty:** affect my reputation for proper maidenly behavior

67. **die the death:** be put to death

69. **question:** examine carefully

70. **Know of:** learn from; **blood:** passions, feelings

72. **livery of a nun:** a nun's distinctive clothing The term *nun* was used by writers in Shakespeare's day to refer not only to Christian nuns but also to pagan virgins dedicated to a life of chaste service to Diana or Vesta. (See page 12.)

73. **For aye:** forever; **mewed:** caged (A mew was a cage for hawks.)

75. **Chanting . . . moon:** Diana was both the moon goddess and the goddess of chastity.

76–77. **Thrice-blessèd . . . pilgrimage:** i.e., those who master their passions and live as chaste maidens separated from the world are **thrice-blessèd**

78–80. **But earthlier . . . blessedness:** i.e., those who marry have more happiness on this earth than those who live and die in **single blessedness**. (The image is of the married woman as a **rose distilled** [plucked and its fragrance distilled into perfume] as opposed to the rose that remains unplucked.)

To whom you are but as a form in wax   50
By him imprinted, and within his power
To leave the figure or disfigure it.
Demetrius is a worthy gentleman.
HERMIA
So is Lysander.
THESEUS   In himself he is,   55
But in this kind, wanting your father's voice,
The other must be held the worthier.
HERMIA
I would my father looked but with my eyes.
THESEUS
Rather your eyes must with his judgment look.
HERMIA
I do entreat your Grace to pardon me.   60
I know not by what power I am made bold,
Nor how it may concern my modesty
In such a presence here to plead my thoughts;
But I beseech your Grace that I may know
The worst that may befall me in this case   65
If I refuse to wed Demetrius.
THESEUS
Either to die the death, or to abjure
Forever the society of men.
Therefore, fair Hermia, question your desires,
Know of your youth, examine well your blood,   70
Whether (if you yield not to your father's choice)
You can endure the livery of a nun,
For aye to be in shady cloister mewed,
To live a barren sister all your life,
Chanting faint hymns to the cold fruitless moon.   75
Thrice-blessèd they that master so their blood
To undergo such maiden pilgrimage,
But earthlier happy is the rose distilled
Than that which, withering on the virgin thorn,
Grows, lives, and dies in single blessedness.   80

82. **my virgin patent:** my entitlement to my virginity; my freedom to live as a virgin.
83. **Unto his lordship:** i.e., to the mastery of a man
90. **he would:** i.e., your father wishes
91. **protest:** vow
92. **austerity:** i.e., a life of self-denial
94. **crazèd title:** flawed claim
96. **Do you:** i.e., you
100. **estate unto:** give to
101. **derived:** born, descended
102. **well possessed:** i.e., wealthy
103. **fairly:** attractively
104. **with vantage:** i.e., even more (than his)
108. **avouch . . . head:** declare it to his face
109. **Made love to:** courted

"The livery of a nun." (1.1.72)
From Johann Basilius Herold, *Heydenwelt . . .* (1554).

HERMIA
  So will I grow, so live, so die, my lord,
  Ere I will yield my virgin patent up
  Unto his lordship whose unwishèd yoke
  My soul consents not to give sovereignty.
THESEUS
  Take time to pause, and by the next new moon   85
  (The sealing day betwixt my love and me
  For everlasting bond of fellowship),
  Upon that day either prepare to die
  For disobedience to your father's will,
  Or else to wed Demetrius, as he would,   90
  Or on Diana's altar to protest
  For aye austerity and single life.
DEMETRIUS
  Relent, sweet Hermia, and, Lysander, yield
  Thy crazèd title to my certain right.
LYSANDER
  You have her father's love, Demetrius.   95
  Let me have Hermia's. Do you marry him.
EGEUS
  Scornful Lysander, true, he hath my love;
  And what is mine my love shall render him.
  And she is mine, and all my right of her
  I do estate unto Demetrius.   100
LYSANDER, ⌜*to Theseus*⌝
  I am, my lord, as well derived as he,
  As well possessed. My love is more than his;
  My fortunes every way as fairly ranked
  (If not with vantage) as Demetrius';
  And (which is more than all these boasts can be)   105
  I am beloved of beauteous Hermia.
  Why should not I then prosecute my right?
  Demetrius, I'll avouch it to his head,
  Made love to Nedar's daughter, Helena,
  And won her soul; and she, sweet lady, dotes,   110

112. **spotted:** i.e., morally stained, wicked

115. **self-affairs:** personal business

118. **schooling:** reproof, admonition

119. **arm:** prepare

122. **by no means we may extenuate:** i.e., I (speaking in my formal capacity) can in no way lessen or change

124. **What cheer . . . ?:** i.e., how are you? (literally, what is your mood or disposition?)

127. **Against:** in preparation for

128. **nearly that concerns yourselves:** i.e., that concerns you closely

131. **How chance . . . ?:** i.e., how does it happen that . . . ?

132. **Belike:** probably; **want:** lack

133. **Beteem:** grant, give

134. **For aught:** according to anything

137. **different in blood:** unequal in hereditary rank

138. **cross:** bar, barrier, obstruction

139. **misgraffèd . . . years:** mismatched in age

Devoutly dotes, dotes in idolatry,
Upon this spotted and inconstant man.
THESEUS
I must confess that I have heard so much,
And with Demetrius thought to have spoke thereof;
But, being overfull of self-affairs,   115
My mind did lose it.—But, Demetrius, come,
And come, Egeus; you shall go with me.
I have some private schooling for you both.—
For you, fair Hermia, look you arm yourself
To fit your fancies to your father's will,   120
Or else the law of Athens yields you up
(Which by no means we may extenuate)
To death or to a vow of single life.—
Come, my Hippolyta. What cheer, my love?—
Demetrius and Egeus, go along.   125
I must employ you in some business
Against our nuptial, and confer with you
Of something nearly that concerns yourselves.
EGEUS
With duty and desire we follow you.
                    ⌜*All but Hermia and Lysander*⌝ *exit.*
LYSANDER
How now, my love? Why is your cheek so pale?   130
How chance the roses there do fade so fast?
HERMIA
Belike for want of rain, which I could well
Beteem them from the tempest of my eyes.
LYSANDER
Ay me! For aught that I could ever read,
Could ever hear by tale or history,   135
The course of true love never did run smooth.
But either it was different in blood—
HERMIA
O cross! Too high to be enthralled to ⌜low.⌝
LYSANDER
Or else misgraffèd in respect of years—

141. **stood upon:** depended on
143. **if . . . choice:** i.e., if the lovers were suitably matched
145. **momentany:** lasting but a moment; instantaneous
147. **collied:** coal-black
148. **That:** the lightning; **in a spleen:** i.e., suddenly, in an impulsive action (The spleen was regarded as the seat of angry impulsiveness.); **unfolds:** reveals
149. **ere:** before
151. **quick:** (1) living, intense; (2) quickly; **confusion:** ruin, defeat
152. **ever crossed:** always frustrated or thwarted
157. **fancy's:** love's
158. **A good persuasion:** i.e., a good attitude for us to take
160. **revenue:** accented here on the second syllable
162. **respects me as:** i.e., regards me as much as if I were
166. **forth:** i.e., forth from
167. **without:** outside of
169. **To do . . . May:** i.e., to celebrate May Day (perhaps by collecting branches and flowers)

HERMIA
  O spite! Too old to be engaged to young.   140
LYSANDER
  Or else it stood upon the choice of friends—
HERMIA
  O hell, to choose love by another's eyes!
LYSANDER
  Or, if there were a sympathy in choice,
  War, death, or sickness did lay siege to it,
  Making it momentany as a sound,   145
  Swift as a shadow, short as any dream,
  Brief as the lightning in the collied night,
  That, in a spleen, unfolds both heaven and earth,
  And, ere a man hath power to say "Behold!"
  The jaws of darkness do devour it up.   150
  So quick bright things come to confusion.
HERMIA
  If then true lovers have been ever crossed,
  It stands as an edict in destiny.
  Then let us teach our trial patience
  Because it is a customary cross,   155
  As due to love as thoughts and dreams and sighs,
  Wishes and tears, poor fancy's followers.
LYSANDER
  A good persuasion. Therefore, hear me, Hermia:
  I have a widow aunt, a dowager
  Of great revenue, and she hath no child.   160
  From Athens is her house remote seven leagues,
  And she respects me as her only son.
  There, gentle Hermia, may I marry thee;
  And to that place the sharp Athenian law
  Cannot pursue us. If thou lovest me, then   165
  Steal forth thy father's house tomorrow night,
  And in the wood a league without the town
  (Where I did meet thee once with Helena
  To do observance to a morn of May),
  There will I stay for thee.   170

173. **arrow with the golden head:** Cupid, the mythological god of love, was said to use arrows with golden heads to cause love, and arrows with leaden heads to repel love.

174. **simplicity:** innocence; **Venus' doves:** Doves were sacred to Venus (goddess of love and mother of Cupid) and were sometimes pictured as drawing her chariot. (See page 46.)

176–77. **that fire . . . was seen:** Dido, queen of Carthage, both burned with love for Aeneas and burned herself on a pyre after Aeneas, **the false Trojan**, abandoned her by sailing off to found Rome.

183. **Godspeed:** a conventional greeting

185. **your fair:** your fairness, beauty; **happy:** fortunate

186. **lodestars:** stars (like the polestar) that sailors used to guide them

187. **tunable:** melodious

189. **catching:** contagious; **favor:** looks

190. **catch:** get as if by infection

194–95. **Demetrius . . . translated:** i.e., I'd give all the world, except for Demetrius, in order to be transformed into you **bated:** excepted, omitted **translated:** transformed

HERMIA   My good Lysander,
  I swear to thee by Cupid's strongest bow,
  By his best arrow with the golden head,
  By the simplicity of Venus' doves,
  By that which knitteth souls and prospers loves,   175
  And by that fire which burned the Carthage queen
  When the false Trojan under sail was seen,
  By all the vows that ever men have broke
  (In number more than ever women spoke),
  In that same place thou hast appointed me,   180
  Tomorrow truly will I meet with thee.
LYSANDER
  Keep promise, love. Look, here comes Helena.

                   Enter Helena.

HERMIA
  Godspeed, fair Helena. Whither away?
HELENA
  Call you me "fair"? That "fair" again unsay.
  Demetrius loves your fair. O happy fair!   185
  Your eyes are lodestars and your tongue's sweet air
  More tunable than lark to shepherd's ear
  When wheat is green, when hawthorn buds appear.
  Sickness is catching. O, were favor so!
  ⌜Yours would⌝ I catch, fair Hermia, ere I go.   190
  My ear should catch your voice, my eye your eye;
  My tongue should catch your tongue's sweet
    melody.
  Were the world mine, Demetrius being bated,
  The rest ⌜I'd⌝ give to be to you translated.   195
  O, teach me how you look and with what art
  You sway the motion of Demetrius' heart!
HERMIA
  I frown upon him, yet he loves me still.
HELENA
  O, that your frowns would teach my smiles such
    skill!   200

206. **Would:** i.e., I wish

211. **what graces . . . dwell:** i.e., how much attractiveness lies in Lysander

214. **Phoebe:** i.e., the moon (Phoebe is another name for Diana, goddess of the moon.)

215. **wat'ry glass:** i.e., pond or lake, which acts as a **glass** or mirror

217. **still:** always

220. **faint:** pale; **wont:** accustomed

224. **stranger companies:** i.e., the company of strangers

Phoebe. (1.1.214)
From Johann Engel, *Astrolabium* (1488).

HERMIA
I give him curses, yet he gives me love.
HELENA
O, that my prayers could such affection move!
HERMIA
The more I hate, the more he follows me.
HELENA
The more I love, the more he hateth me.
HERMIA
His folly, Helena, is no fault of mine.   205
HELENA
None but your beauty. Would that fault were mine!
HERMIA
Take comfort: he no more shall see my face.
Lysander and myself will fly this place.
Before the time I did Lysander see
Seemed Athens as a paradise to me.   210
O, then, what graces in my love do dwell
That he hath turned a heaven unto a hell!
LYSANDER
Helen, to you our minds we will unfold.
Tomorrow night when Phoebe doth behold
Her silver visage in the wat'ry glass,   215
Decking with liquid pearl the bladed grass
(A time that lovers' flights doth still conceal),
Through Athens' gates have we devised to steal.
HERMIA
And in the wood where often you and I
Upon faint primrose beds were wont to lie,   220
Emptying our bosoms of their counsel ⌐sweet,⌐
There my Lysander and myself shall meet,
And thence from Athens turn away our eyes
To seek new friends and ⌐stranger companies.⌐
Farewell, sweet playfellow. Pray thou for us,   225
And good luck grant thee thy Demetrius.—

228. **lovers' food:** i.e., the sight of each other

232. **o'er other some:** i.e., in comparison to certain others

238. **holding no quantity:** i.e., out of all proportion

240–47. **Love . . . everywhere:** Helena uses the ways in which Cupid is often pictured (as a blind boy with wings) to describe the qualities of love—its blindness, lack of judgment, folly, and inconstancy. (See page 114.)

242. **of any judgment taste:** i.e., any taste of judgment

243. **figure:** represent; **unheedy:** heedless, reckless

245. **beguiled:** cheated

246. **game:** sport; **forswear:** swear falsely, perjure

247. **is perjured:** i.e., perjures himself

248. **eyne:** eyes

249. **hailed down:** showered, poured down like hail

254. **intelligence:** news

255. **If . . . expense:** Helena may be saying that she is purchasing Demetrius's thanks at great cost; or, she may mean that her efforts will be dear to her if they bring her Demetrius's thanks. **dear:** (1) high priced; (2) loved, precious

Keep word, Lysander. We must starve our sight
From lovers' food till morrow deep midnight.
LYSANDER
  I will, my Hermia.   *Hermia exits.*
               Helena, adieu.   230
  As you on him, Demetrius dote on you!
                              Lysander exits.

HELENA
  How happy some o'er other some can be!
  Through Athens I am thought as fair as she.
  But what of that? Demetrius thinks not so.
  He will not know what all but he do know.   235
  And, as he errs, doting on Hermia's eyes,
  So I, admiring of his qualities.
  Things base and vile, holding no quantity,
  Love can transpose to form and dignity.
  Love looks not with the eyes but with the mind;   240
  And therefore is winged Cupid painted blind.
  Nor hath Love's mind of any judgment taste.
  Wings, and no eyes, figure unheedy haste.
  And therefore is Love said to be a child
  Because in choice he is so oft beguiled.   245
  As waggish boys in game themselves forswear,
  So the boy Love is perjured everywhere.
  For, ere Demetrius looked on Hermia's eyne,
  He hailed down oaths that he was only mine;
  And when this hail some heat from Hermia felt,   250
  So he dissolved, and show'rs of oaths did melt.
  I will go tell him of fair Hermia's flight.
  Then to the wood will he tomorrow night
  Pursue her. And, for this intelligence
  If I have thanks, it is a dear expense.   255
  But herein mean I to enrich my pain,
  To have his sight thither and back again.
                              She exits.

1.2 Six Athenian tradesmen decide to put on a play, called "Pyramus and Thisbe," for Theseus and Hippolyta's wedding. Pyramus will be played by Bottom the weaver and Thisbe by Francis Flute the bellows-mender. The men are given their parts to study, and they agree to meet for a rehearsal in the woods outside Athens.

---

0 SD. **joiner:** carpenter, cabinetmaker

2. **You were best:** i.e., you had better; **generally:** Bottom's mistake for "individually"

3. **scrip:** a piece of paper with writing on it

4. **which:** i.e., who

6. **interlude:** an entertainment that comes between other events (here, a play to fill the time between the wedding and bedtime)

10. **grow to a point:** As in many of Bottom's lines, one gets a sense of what he means even though he uses language oddly. Here, he seems to mean "come to a conclusion."

11. **Marry:** i.e., indeed (originally an oath on the name of the Virgin Mary)

12–13. **Pyramus and Thisbe:** The story of Pyramus and Thisbe—a story very much like that of Romeo and Juliet—is told in Ovid's *Metamorphoses,* book IV.

23. **ask:** require

25. **condole:** grieve, lament (Bottom probably means that he will act the part of the grieving lover.)

26. **humor:** inclination, preference

27. **Ercles:** Hercules (This may be an allusion to a lost play about the Greek hero; or, the role of Her-

(continued)

⌈Scene 2⌉

Enter Quince the carpenter, and Snug the joiner, and
Bottom the weaver, and Flute the bellows-mender, and
Snout the tinker, and Starveling the tailor.

QUINCE   Is all our company here?

BOTTOM   You were best to call them generally, man by
man, according to the scrip.

QUINCE   Here is the scroll of every man's name which
is thought fit, through all Athens, to play in our   5
interlude before the Duke and the Duchess on his
wedding day at night.

BOTTOM   First, good Peter Quince, say what the play
treats on, then read the names of the actors, and so
grow to a point.   10

QUINCE   Marry, our play is "The most lamentable
comedy and most cruel death of Pyramus and
Thisbe."

BOTTOM   A very good piece of work, I assure you, and a
merry. Now, good Peter Quince, call forth your   15
actors by the scroll. Masters, spread yourselves.

QUINCE   Answer as I call you. Nick Bottom, the weaver.

BOTTOM   Ready. Name what part I am for, and proceed.

QUINCE   You, Nick Bottom, are set down for Pyramus.   20

BOTTOM   What is Pyramus—a lover or a tyrant?

QUINCE   A lover that kills himself most gallant for love.

BOTTOM   That will ask some tears in the true performing of it. If I do it, let the audience look to their
eyes. I will move storms; I will condole in some   25
measure. To the rest.—Yet my chief humor is for a
tyrant. I could play Ercles rarely, or a part to tear a
cat in, to make all split:

> *The raging rocks*
> *And shivering shocks*   30
> *Shall break the locks*

cules may have been famous as an extravagant, ranting part.)

27–28. **tear a cat:** i.e., rant and rave

33. **Phibbus' car:** the chariot of the sun god, Phoebus Apollo

38. **Ercles' vein:** the style of Hercules (See note on line 27, above.)

42. **take . . . on you:** i.e., play the part of

43. **wand'ring knight:** knight-errant (i.e., a hero's role in medieval romance)

47. **That's all one:** i.e., no matter; **mask:** perhaps alluding to the masks that women frequently wore when out of doors to protect their skin from the sun

48. **small:** shrill, high-pitched

49. **An:** i.e., if

50. **monstrous little:** extremely small

"Phibbus' car." (1.2.33)
From Hyginus, *Fabularum liber* (1549).

> *Of prison gates.*
> *And Phibbus' car*
> *Shall shine from far*
> *And make and mar*   35
> *The foolish Fates.*

This was lofty. Now name the rest of the players.
This is Ercles' vein, a tyrant's vein. A lover is more
condoling.

QUINCE   Francis Flute, the bellows-mender.   40

FLUTE   Here, Peter Quince.

QUINCE   Flute, you must take Thisbe on you.

FLUTE   What is Thisbe—a wand'ring knight?

QUINCE   It is the lady that Pyramus must love.

FLUTE   Nay, faith, let not me play a woman. I have a   45
beard coming.

QUINCE   That's all one. You shall play it in a mask, and
you may speak as small as you will.

BOTTOM   An I may hide my face, let me play Thisbe too.
I'll speak in a monstrous little voice: "Thisne,   50
Thisne!"—"Ah Pyramus, my lover dear! Thy Thisbe
dear and lady dear!"

QUINCE   No, no, you must play Pyramus—and, Flute,
you Thisbe.

BOTTOM   Well, proceed.   55

QUINCE   Robin Starveling, the tailor.

STARVELING   Here, Peter Quince.

QUINCE   Robin Starveling, you must play Thisbe's
mother.—Tom Snout, the tinker.

SNOUT   Here, Peter Quince.   60

QUINCE   You, Pyramus' father.—Myself, Thisbe's
father.—Snug the joiner, you the lion's part.—
And I hope here is a play fitted.

SNUG   Have you the lion's part written? Pray you, if it
be, give it me, for I am slow of study.   65

QUINCE   You may do it extempore, for it is nothing but
roaring.

74. **were:** i.e., would be

78. **discretion:** judgment (Bottom seems to mean that they would have no choice but to hang them.); **aggravate:** Bottom's mistake for "moderate" or "mitigate" (i.e., soften, tone down)

79. **roar you:** i.e., roar for you;

79–80. **sucking dove:** Bottom's confusion of "sucking [i.e., unweaned] lamb" and "sitting [i.e., hatching] dove"

80. **an 'twere:** as if it were

82. **a proper:** i.e., as handsome a

84. **must needs:** i.e., must

88. **will:** i.e., wish

89. **discharge:** perform; **your:** i.e., a (a colloquialism)

90. **orange-tawny:** tan

90–91. **purple-in-grain:** crimson fast-dyed

91. **French-crown:** gold (the color of the French coin called a "crown" in English)

92. **perfit:** perfect (Since "perfect" became the preferred spelling around 1590, it is possible that the old form was deliberately chosen for Bottom—as again at line 105.)

93–94. **French . . . all:** an allusion to the baldness caused by syphilis (the "French disease")

96. **con:** learn

98. **without:** outside of

100. **devices:** plans; or, the plot of our play (The word *device* was sometimes used to denote a play or masque—as it is in Act 5 of this play.)

101. **bill of properties:** list of stage props

BOTTOM   Let me play the lion too. I will roar that I will
   do any man's heart good to hear me. I will roar that
   I will make the Duke say "Let him roar again. Let   70
   him roar again!"

QUINCE   An you should do it too terribly, you would
   fright the Duchess and the ladies that they would
   shriek, and that were enough to hang us all.

ALL   That would hang us, every mother's son.   75

BOTTOM   I grant you, friends, if you should fright the
   ladies out of their wits, they would have no more
   discretion but to hang us. But I will aggravate my
   voice so that I will roar you as gently as any sucking
   dove. I will roar you an 'twere any nightingale.   80

QUINCE   You can play no part but Pyramus, for Pyramus is a sweet-faced man, a proper man as one
   shall see in a summer's day, a most lovely gentle-
   manlike man. Therefore you must needs play Pyramus.   85

BOTTOM   Well, I will undertake it. What beard were I
   best to play it in?

QUINCE   Why, what you will.

BOTTOM   I will discharge it in either your straw-color
   beard, your orange-tawny beard, your purple-   90
   in-grain beard, or your French-crown-color beard,
   your perfit yellow.

QUINCE   Some of your French crowns have no hair at
   all, and then you will play barefaced. But, masters,
   here are your parts, ⌜*giving out the parts,*⌝ and I am   95
   to entreat you, request you, and desire you, to con
   them by tomorrow night and meet me in the palace
   wood, a mile without the town, by moonlight. There
   will we rehearse, for if we meet in the city, we shall
   be dogged with company and our devices known. In   100
   the meantime I will draw a bill of properties such as
   our play wants. I pray you fail me not.

BOTTOM   We will meet, and there we may rehearse

104. **obscenely:** Bottom perhaps means "seemly."

105. **perfit:** i.e., word-perfect

107. **Hold, or cut bowstrings:** This sounds like a proverb, or like an archery term, but seems to be Bottom's invention. (Perhaps it means "Keep your word or be disgraced.")

most obscenely and courageously. Take pains. Be
perfit. Adieu.   105
QUINCE   At the Duke's Oak we meet.
BOTTOM   Enough. Hold, or cut bowstrings.

They exit.

A
MIDSUMMER
NIGHT'S DREAM

ACT 2

2.1 Oberon and Titania, king and queen of the fairies, quarrel over possession of a young Indian boy. Oberon orders Robin Goodfellow, a hobgoblin or "puck," to obtain a special flower that makes people fall in love with the next creature they see. Oberon wants to make Titania fall in love with a beast and use her infatuation to get the Indian boy from her. Demetrius enters pursued by Helena, whom he tries to drive off. When Robin returns, Oberon, who sympathizes with Helena's love, orders him to find the Athenian man (i.e., Demetrius) and apply some of the flower's magic nectar to his eyes.

---

0 SD. **Robin Goodfellow:** a "puck," or mischievous spirit, whose activities are described in lines 33–59 (Since Nicholas Rowe's 1709 edition of the play, the character has been known as "Puck.") Robin appears in stories, plays, and books on witchcraft, sometimes as simply mischievous, sometimes as an evil goblin. (See page 58.)

3. **Thorough:** i.e., through

4. **pale:** fenced-in area

7. **moon's sphere:** In Ptolemaic astronomy, the moon (like the planets, the stars, and the sun) was carried around the earth in a crystalline sphere.

9. **orbs:** circles (A circle of darker, more luxuriant, grass in a meadow was called a "fairy ring" and was thought to be the dancing ground of fairies.)

10. **pensioners:** Because of their height and their brightly colored flowers (gold with ruby-red spots), **cowslips** are compared to the gaudily dressed bodyguards (**pensioners**) that served Queen Elizabeth.

16. **lob:** oaf, lout

(continued)

⎯⎯⎯⎯⎯⎯⎯⎯⎯⎯⎯⎯⎯⎯⎯⎯⎯⎯⎯⎯

⌜Scene 1⌝
*Enter a Fairy at one door and Robin Goodfellow at
another.*

ROBIN
How now, spirit? Whither wander you?
FAIRY
    Over hill, over dale,
      Thorough bush, thorough brier,
    Over park, over pale,
      Thorough flood, thorough fire;   5
    I do wander everywhere,
    Swifter than the moon's sphere.
    And I serve the Fairy Queen,
    To dew her orbs upon the green.
    The cowslips tall her pensioners be;   10
    In their gold coats spots you see;
    Those be rubies, fairy favors;
    In those freckles live their savors.
I must go seek some dewdrops here
And hang a pearl in every cowslip's ear.   15
Farewell, thou lob of spirits. I'll be gone.
Our queen and all her elves come here anon.
ROBIN
The King doth keep his revels here tonight.
Take heed the Queen come not within his sight,

17. **anon:** soon

18. **revels:** At the court of Queen Elizabeth, **revels** were presented at special seasons, and included plays, masques, and sports. Here, the king of fairyland's **revels** might also include dancing.

20. **passing:** i.e., surpassingly, extremely; **fell and wrath:** i.e., fiercely angry

25. **trace:** travel through

26. **perforce:** forcibly

29. **they:** i.e., the king and queen of fairies

30. **fountain:** spring

31. **square:** quarrel; **that:** i.e., so that

34. **shrewd:** mischievous, malicious; **sprite:** spirit

35. **Robin Goodfellow:** See the note on 2.1.0 SD.

36. **villagery:** villages

37. **Skim milk:** i.e., steal the cream from the milk; **labor in the quern:** i.e., work at the quern (a small mill for grinding corn), to frustrate the grinding

38. **bootless . . . churn:** i.e., make her churning produce no butter **bootless:** uselessly, fruitlessly **huswife:** pronounced "hussif"

39. **barm:** yeasty "head" on beer.

47. **beguile:** deceive, trick

49. **gossip's bowl:** the cup from which the gossiping or tattling woman is drinking

50. **crab:** crab apple (Roasted crabapples and spices were added to hot ale to make a winter drink.)

52. **dewlap:** the fold of skin hanging from the neck of certain animals (here applied to the neck of the old woman)

53. **aunt:** perhaps, old woman or gossip; **telling . . . tale:** "Winter's tales" and "old wives' tales," told to while away long evenings, could be merry or sad.

For Oberon is passing fell and wrath   20
Because that she, as her attendant, hath
A lovely boy stolen from an Indian king;
She never had so sweet a changeling.
And jealous Oberon would have the child
Knight of his train, to trace the forests wild.   25
But she perforce withholds the lovèd boy,
Crowns him with flowers, and makes him all her
    joy.
And now they never meet in grove or green,
By fountain clear, or spangled starlight sheen,   30
But they do square, that all their elves for fear
Creep into acorn cups and hide them there.

FAIRY
Either I mistake your shape and making quite,
Or else you are that shrewd and knavish sprite
Called Robin Goodfellow. Are not you he   35
That frights the maidens of the villagery,
Skim milk, and sometimes labor in the quern
And bootless make the breathless huswife churn,
And sometime make the drink to bear no barm,
Mislead night wanderers, laughing at their harm?   40
Those that "Hobgoblin" call you, and "sweet Puck,"
You do their work, and they shall have good luck.
Are not you he?

ROBIN   Thou speakest aright.
I am that merry wanderer of the night.   45
I jest to Oberon and make him smile
When I a fat and bean-fed horse beguile,
Neighing in likeness of a filly foal.
And sometime lurk I in a gossip's bowl
In very likeness of a roasted crab,   50
And, when she drinks, against her lips I bob
And on her withered dewlap pour the ale.
The wisest aunt, telling the saddest tale,
Sometime for three-foot stool mistaketh me;

56. **"Tailor":** Since "tail" could mean "buttocks," it has been suggested that the old woman's cry might be translated as "O my bum!" (It remains uncertain just what the expression means.)

57. **choir:** company

57–58. **loffe . . . waxen . . . neeze:** These archaic forms of "laugh," "wax" (i.e., increase), and "sneeze" seem to reproduce the country setting Robin is describing.

60. **room:** i.e., make room, stand aside

64. **forsworn:** renounced, formally rejected

65. **rash wanton:** foolish rebel; **lord:** husband (and therefore having the right to control his wife)

66. **lady:** wife (and therefore having the right to expect her husband to be faithful)

68. **in . . . Corin:** disguised as a lovesick shepherd

69. **of corn:** i.e., made from wheat straws

70. **Phillida:** traditional shepherdess of love poetry

71. **steep:** slope, cliff

72. **forsooth:** in truth, certainly; **Amazon:** In stories about Theseus, Hippolyta was one of the Amazon warriors (a tribe of women fighters) who attacked Athens. After four months of fighting, peace was reached through Hippolyta's efforts.

73. **buskined:** wearing buskins, or boots

74. **must be:** i.e., is to be

75. **their bed:** i.e., their marriage and offspring

77. **Glance at:** allude to; **credit:** reputation

81–83. **Perigouna . . . Aegles . . . Ariadne . . . Antiopa:** In stories about Theseus, these are lovers whom Theseus deserted. Oberon lays the blame for these desertions on Titania. **break . . . faith:** i.e., go back on his word, break his promise

Then slip I from her bum, down topples she,   55
And "Tailor!" cries, and falls into a cough,
And then the whole choir hold their hips and loffe
And waxen in their mirth and neeze and swear
A merrier hour was never wasted there.
But room, fairy. Here comes Oberon.   60

FAIRY
And here my mistress. Would that he were gone!

Enter ⌜*Oberon*⌝ *the King of Fairies at one door, with his*
train, and ⌜*Titania*⌝ *the Queen at another, with hers.*

OBERON
Ill met by moonlight, proud Titania.

TITANIA
What, jealous Oberon? ⌜Fairies,⌝ skip hence.
I have forsworn his bed and company.

OBERON
Tarry, rash wanton. Am not I thy lord?   65

TITANIA
Then I must be thy lady. But I know
When thou hast stolen away from Fairyland
And in the shape of Corin sat all day
Playing on pipes of corn and versing love
To amorous Phillida. Why art thou here,   70
Come from the farthest steep of India,
But that, forsooth, the bouncing Amazon,
Your buskined mistress and your warrior love,
To Theseus must be wedded, and you come
To give their bed joy and prosperity?   75

OBERON
How canst thou thus for shame, Titania,
Glance at my credit with Hippolyta,
Knowing I know thy love to Theseus?
Didst not thou lead him through the glimmering
    night   80
From ⌜Perigouna,⌝ whom he ravishèd,

84. **forgeries:** fictions, fictitious inventions

85. **middle summer's spring:** i.e., the beginning of midsummer

86. **mead:** meadow

87. **pavèd:** pebbled

88. **margent:** margin

89. **ringlets:** circle dances

91. **piping:** i.e., whistling, making music

94. **pelting:** paltry, insignificant

95. **continents:** i.e., banks (which contain them)

97–98. **green corn . . . beard:** As grain (called, in England, corn) ripens, its head develops bristle-like extensions; it is then called "bearded."

99. **fold:** i.e., sheepfold, or pen

100. **murrain flock:** i.e., sheep dead from murrain, an infectious disease

101. **nine-men's-morris:** an outdoor space carved, or cut in turf, for a game of the same name

102. **quaint:** elaborate; **mazes:** intricate interconnecting paths that lead confusingly to (and away from) a center; **wanton green:** luxuriant grass

103. **tread:** perhaps, human footsteps which, when tracing the maze, would keep its path clear; **undistinguishable:** not perceptible

104. **want:** lack

106. **Therefore:** i.e., (as in line 91) because of Oberon's disturbance of the fairy dances

108. **That:** i.e., so that; **rheumatic:** i.e., like colds or flu, with discharges of rheum or mucus (accent on first syllable)

109. **thorough:** i.e., through, as a consequence of; **distemperature:** (1) bad temper; (2) bad weather

112. **Hiems':** i.e., winter's

(continued)

And make him with fair ⌜Aegles⌝ break his faith,
With Ariadne and Antiopa?

TITANIA
These are the forgeries of jealousy;
And never, since the middle summer's spring,   85
Met we on hill, in dale, forest, or mead,
By pavèd fountain or by rushy brook,
Or in the beachèd margent of the sea,
To dance our ringlets to the whistling wind,
But with thy brawls thou hast disturbed our sport.   90
Therefore the winds, piping to us in vain,
As in revenge have sucked up from the sea
Contagious fogs, which, falling in the land,
Hath every pelting river made so proud
That they have overborne their continents.   95
The ox hath therefore stretched his yoke in vain,
The plowman lost his sweat, and the green corn
Hath rotted ere his youth attained a beard.
The fold stands empty in the drownèd field,
And crows are fatted with the murrain flock.   100
The nine-men's-morris is filled up with mud,
And the quaint mazes in the wanton green,
For lack of tread, are undistinguishable.
The human mortals want their winter here.
No night is now with hymn or carol blessed.   105
Therefore the moon, the governess of floods,
Pale in her anger, washes all the air,
That rheumatic diseases do abound.
And thorough this distemperature we see
The seasons alter: hoary-headed frosts   110
Fall in the fresh lap of the crimson rose,
And on old Hiems' ⌜thin⌝ and icy crown
An odorous chaplet of sweet summer buds
Is, as in mockery, set. The spring, the summer,
The childing autumn, angry winter, change   115
Their wonted liveries, and the mazèd world

113. **odorous:** fragrant

115. **childing:** fruitful (producing "children"); **change:** exchange

116. **wonted liveries:** usual outfits

116–17. **the mazèd world . . . which:** i.e., the bewildered world can no longer distinguish one season from another according to the produce (**increase**) normally brought forth in each   **mazèd:** bewildered

118–19. **this same . . . debate:** these evils are the descendants of our quarrel   **debate:** quarrel

120. **original:** origin

122. **cross:** oppose, resist

124. **henchman:** page, squire

127. **vot'ress . . . order:** woman vowed to serve me

129. **Full:** i.e., very

130. **Neptune:** the god of the sea (See page 110.)

131. **Marking:** noticing, watching; **embarkèd . . . flood:** i.e., merchant ships sailing on the ocean

133. **wanton:** (1) lewd; (2) playful

145. **round:** circle dance

147. **spare your haunts:** avoid the places you frequent

By their increase now knows not which is which.
And this same progeny of evils comes
From our debate, from our dissension;
We are their parents and original.   120
OBERON
Do you amend it, then. It lies in you.
Why should Titania cross her Oberon?
I do but beg a little changeling boy
To be my henchman.
TITANIA   Set your heart at rest: 125
The Fairyland buys not the child of me.
His mother was a vot'ress of my order,
And in the spicèd Indian air by night
Full often hath she gossiped by my side
And sat with me on Neptune's yellow sands,   130
Marking th' embarkèd traders on the flood,
When we have laughed to see the sails conceive
And grow big-bellied with the wanton wind;
Which she, with pretty and with swimming gait,
Following (her womb then rich with my young   135
   squire),
Would imitate and sail upon the land
To fetch me trifles and return again,
As from a voyage, rich with merchandise.
But she, being mortal, of that boy did die,   140
And for her sake do I rear up her boy,
And for her sake I will not part with him.
OBERON
How long within this wood intend you stay?
TITANIA
Perchance till after Theseus' wedding day.
If you will patiently dance in our round   145
And see our moonlight revels, go with us.
If not, shun me, and I will spare your haunts.
OBERON
Give me that boy and I will go with thee.

150. **chide:** fight, brawl; **downright:** i.e., outright

151. **from:** i.e., go from

152. **injury:** wrong, insult

154. **Since:** i.e., when

158. **stars . . . spheres:** See note on 2.1.7, above

164. **vestal:** i.e., virgin (This passage is often explained as referring to Queen Elizabeth I.)

165. **smartly:** briskly

166. **As:** i.e., as if

167. **might:** i.e., could

168. **wat'ry moon:** Because the moon controls the tides, it is often associated with water.

169. **imperial:** commanding, majestic; perhaps also (as a reference to Queen Elizabeth) pertaining to rulership of an empire (In the 1596 edition of Spenser's *Faerie Queene,* for example, Spenser refers to "The Most . . . Magnificent Empresse . . . Elizabeth . . . Queene of England, France and Ireland and of Virginia. . . ."); **vot'ress:** a woman under a vow (The word **vestal** suggests it is a vow of chastity.)

171. **bolt:** arrow

174. **love-in-idleness:** a name for the pansy or heartsease

175. **herb:** plant

177. **or . . . or:** either . . . or

180. **leviathan:** a monstrous sea creature mentioned in the Bible; **league:** approximately three miles

TITANIA
　Not for thy fairy kingdom. Fairies, away.
　We shall chide downright if I longer stay.　　　150
　　　　　　　⌜*Titania and her fairies*⌝ *exit.*
OBERON
　Well, go thy way. Thou shalt not from this grove
　Till I torment thee for this injury.—
　My gentle Puck, come hither. Thou rememb'rest
　Since once I sat upon a promontory
　And heard a mermaid on a dolphin's back　　　155
　Uttering such dulcet and harmonious breath
　That the rude sea grew civil at her song
　And certain stars shot madly from their spheres
　To hear the sea-maid's music.
ROBIN　　　　　　　　　　　I remember.　　　160
OBERON
　That very time I saw (but thou couldst not),
　Flying between the cold moon and the earth,
　Cupid all armed. A certain aim he took
　At a fair vestal thronèd by ⌜the⌝ west,
　And loosed his love-shaft smartly from his bow　　165
　As it should pierce a hundred thousand hearts.
　But I might see young Cupid's fiery shaft
　Quenched in the chaste beams of the wat'ry moon,
　And the imperial vot'ress passèd on
　In maiden meditation, fancy-free.　　　170
　Yet marked I where the bolt of Cupid fell.
　It fell upon a little western flower,
　Before, milk-white, now purple with love's wound,
　And maidens call it "love-in-idleness."
　Fetch me that flower; the herb I showed thee once.　175
　The juice of it on sleeping eyelids laid
　Will make or man or woman madly dote
　Upon the next live creature that it sees.
　Fetch me this herb, and be thou here again
　Ere the leviathan can swim a league.　　　180

183. **juice:** nectar from the flower
192. **page:** boy attending on a knight
197. **stay:** halt, stop; **stayeth:** arrests, holds
199. **and wood:** and mad, insane
202. **adamant:** i.e., like a magnet
203. **draw:** attract
204. **Leave you:** i.e., give up
206. **speak you fair:** i.e., speak to you civilly
208. **nor:** i.e., and

"Venus' doves." (1.1.174)
From Joannes ab Indagine, *The book of palmestry* (1666).

ROBIN
  I'll put a girdle round about the earth
  In forty minutes.   ⌜*He exits.*⌝
OBERON   Having once this juice,
  I'll watch Titania when she is asleep
  And drop the liquor of it in her eyes.   185
  The next thing then she, waking, looks upon
  (Be it on lion, bear, or wolf, or bull,
  On meddling monkey, or on busy ape)
  She shall pursue it with the soul of love.
  And ere I take this charm from off her sight   190
  (As I can take it with another herb),
  I'll make her render up her page to me.
  But who comes here? I am invisible,
  And I will overhear their conference.

            Enter Demetrius, Helena following him.

DEMETRIUS
  I love thee not; therefore pursue me not.   195
  Where is Lysander and fair Hermia?
  The one I'll stay; the other stayeth me.
  Thou told'st me they were stol'n unto this wood,
  And here am I, and wood within this wood
  Because I cannot meet my Hermia.   200
  Hence, get thee gone, and follow me no more.
HELENA
  You draw me, you hard-hearted adamant!
  But yet you draw not iron, for my heart
  Is true as steel. Leave you your power to draw,
  And I shall have no power to follow you.   205
DEMETRIUS
  Do I entice you? Do I speak you fair?
  Or rather do I not in plainest truth
  Tell you I do not, ⌜nor⌝ I cannot love you?
HELENA
  And even for that do I love you the more.

221. **impeach:** call into question, discredit; **modesty:** i.e., properly chaste female behavior

222. **To leave:** i.e., in leaving

225. **ill:** evil; **desert:** uninhabited

227. **virtue:** (1) excellence; (2) moral goodness; **privilege:** i.e., protection; **For that:** i.e., because

231. **For:** because; **in my respect:** i.e., from my perspective

234. **brakes:** thickets

238–40. **Apollo . . . tiger:** Helena gives three examples of stories that are **changed** so that the weak pursue the strong: the chaste nymph Daphne chases the god Apollo (in mythology, Daphne fled from Apollo and escaped him by being transformed into a laurel tree); the dove attacks the mythical beast called the griffin; the female deer chases the tiger. **griffin:** an animal with the head of an eagle on the body of a lion

A griffin. (2.1.239)
From Giulio Cesare Capaccio,
Delle imprese trattato . . . (1592).

I am your spaniel, and, Demetrius,   210
The more you beat me I will fawn on you.
Use me but as your spaniel: spurn me, strike me,
Neglect me, lose me; only give me leave
(Unworthy as I am) to follow you.
What worser place can I beg in your love   215
(And yet a place of high respect with me)
Than to be usèd as you use your dog?

DEMETRIUS
Tempt not too much the hatred of my spirit,
For I am sick when I do look on thee.

HELENA
And I am sick when I look not on you.   220

DEMETRIUS
You do impeach your modesty too much
To leave the city and commit yourself
Into the hands of one that loves you not,
To trust the opportunity of night
And the ill counsel of a desert place   225
With the rich worth of your virginity.

HELENA
Your virtue is my privilege. For that
It is not night when I do see your face,
Therefore I think I am not in the night.
Nor doth this wood lack worlds of company,   230
For you, in my respect, are all the world.
Then, how can it be said I am alone
When all the world is here to look on me?

DEMETRIUS
I'll run from thee and hide me in the brakes
And leave thee to the mercy of wild beasts.   235

HELENA
The wildest hath not such a heart as you.
Run when you will. The story shall be changed:
Apollo flies and Daphne holds the chase;
The dove pursues the griffin; the mild hind

240. **Bootless:** useless, fruitless
242. **stay:** i.e., stay for
243–44. **do . . . But:** i.e., you may be sure that
244, 246. **do . . . mischief:** harm
247. **my sex:** i.e., all females
251. **upon:** by
253. **fly:** flee from
257. **blows:** bursts into flower
258. **oxlips:** flowers somewhat larger than cowslips
259. **woodbine:** honeysuckle (See page 122.)
260. **eglantine:** sweetbrier
261. **sometime of:** sometimes during
263. **throws:** casts; **her:** i.e., its
264. **Weed:** garment
265. **this:** i.e., of the magic flower

Makes speed to catch the tiger. Bootless speed   240
When cowardice pursues and valor flies!

DEMETRIUS
I will not stay thy questions. Let me go,
Or if thou follow me, do not believe
But I shall do thee mischief in the wood.

HELENA
Ay, in the temple, in the town, the field,   245
You do me mischief. Fie, Demetrius!
Your wrongs do set a scandal on my sex.
We cannot fight for love as men may do.
We should be wooed and were not made to woo.
⌜*Demetrius exits.*⌝
I'll follow thee and make a heaven of hell   250
To die upon the hand I love so well.   ⌜*Helena exits.*⌝

OBERON
Fare thee well, nymph. Ere he do leave this grove,
Thou shalt fly him, and he shall seek thy love.

Enter ⌜*Robin.*⌝

Hast thou the flower there? Welcome, wanderer.

ROBIN
Ay, there it is.   255

OBERON   I pray thee give it me.
⌜*Robin gives him the flower.*⌝
I know a bank where the wild thyme blows,
Where oxlips and the nodding violet grows,
Quite overcanopied with luscious woodbine,
With sweet muskroses, and with eglantine.   260
There sleeps Titania sometime of the night,
Lulled in these flowers with dances and delight.
And there the snake throws her enameled skin,
Weed wide enough to wrap a fairy in.
And with the juice of this I'll streak her eyes   265
And make her full of hateful fantasies.
Take thou some of it, and seek through this grove.

273. **that:** i.e., so that

274. **fond on:** desperately in love with

2.2 Oberon anoints Titania's eyes as she sleeps. A weary Lysander and Hermia enter and fall asleep nearby. Robin, thinking he has found "the Athenian man," anoints the eyes of the sleeping Lysander and exits. Demetrius and Helena arrive, and he leaves her behind. Lysander awakes, sees Helena, and immediately falls in love with her. She mistakes his courtship for mockery and tries to elude him. After they exit, the abandoned Hermia awakes from a nightmare and goes in search of her beloved Lysander.

---

1. **roundel:** perhaps, a round dance; or, a song (a "roundelay")

3. **cankers:** canker worms, grubs

4. **reremice:** bats

7. **quaint:** dainty, brisk

8. **offices:** duties, responsibilities

9. **double:** forked

11. **Newts and blindworms:** species of salamanders and reptiles thought, in Shakespeare's day, to be poisonous

13. **Philomel:** the nightingale (named for Philomela, who, in classical mythology, was transformed into a nightingale after she was raped by her brother-in-law and her tongue cut out)

⌜*He gives Robin part of the flower.*⌝
A sweet Athenian lady is in love
With a disdainful youth. Anoint his eyes,
But do it when the next thing he espies   270
May be the lady. Thou shalt know the man
By the Athenian garments he hath on.
Effect it with some care, that he may prove
More fond on her than she upon her love.
And look thou meet me ere the first cock crow.   275

ROBIN
Fear not, my lord. Your servant shall do so.

They exit.

⌜Scene 2⌝
Enter Titania, Queen of Fairies, with her train.

TITANIA
Come, now a roundel and a fairy song;
Then, for the third part of a minute, hence—
Some to kill cankers in the muskrose buds,
Some war with reremice for their leathern wings
To make my small elves coats, and some keep back   5
The clamorous owl that nightly hoots and wonders
At our quaint spirits. Sing me now asleep.
Then to your offices and let me rest.⌜*She lies down.*⌝

Fairies sing.

⌜FIRST FAIRY⌝
You spotted snakes with double tongue,
Thorny hedgehogs, be not seen.   10
Newts and blindworms, do no wrong,
Come not near our Fairy Queen.
⌜CHORUS⌝
Philomel, with melody
Sing in our sweet lullaby.

36. **ounce:** lynx; **cat:** i.e., lion or tiger
37. **Pard:** leopard
38. **that:** i.e., that which

An "ounce." (2.2.36)
From Edward Topsell,
The historie of foure-footed beastes . . . (1607).

> *Lulla, lulla, lullaby, lulla, lulla, lullaby.* 15
>   *Never harm*
>   *Nor spell nor charm*
> *Come our lovely lady nigh.*
>   *So good night, with lullaby.*

FIRST FAIRY
> *Weaving spiders, come not here.* 20
>   *Hence, you long-legged spinners, hence.*
> *Beetles black, approach not near.*
>   *Worm nor snail, do no offence.*

⌈CHORUS⌉
>   *Philomel, with melody*
>   *Sing in our sweet lullaby.* 25
> *Lulla, lulla, lullaby, lulla, lulla, lullaby.*
>   *Never harm*
>   *Nor spell nor charm*
> *Come our lovely lady nigh.*
>   *So good night, with lullaby.* 30
> > > ⌈*Titania sleeps.*⌉

SECOND FAIRY
> Hence, away! Now all is well.
> One aloof stand sentinel.   ⌈*Fairies exit.*⌉

Enter Oberon, ⌈*who anoints Titania's eyelids with the nectar.*⌉

OBERON
> What thou seest when thou dost wake,
> Do it for thy true love take.
> Love and languish for his sake. 35
> Be it ounce, or cat, or bear,
> Pard, or boar with bristled hair,
> In thy eye that shall appear
> When thou wak'st, it is thy dear.
> Wake when some vile thing is near. ⌈*He exits.*⌉ 40

Enter Lysander and Hermia.

42. **troth:** truth, truly

48. **troth:** faithful vow

51. **take . . . innocence:** perhaps, understand the innocent meaning—i.e., of what I just said (In lines 53–58, Lysander explains what he meant in line 48.)

52. **Love . . . conference:** i.e., when lovers talk, it is love that hears and understands

60. **beshrew:** literally, curse (but the harshness of the word was lost through repeated use)

63. **human:** humane, civil, courteous

70. **Here:** Lysander would be some distance from where Hermia is lying.

LYSANDER
 Fair love, you faint with wand'ring in the wood.
  And, to speak troth, I have forgot our way.
 We'll rest us, Hermia, if you think it good,
  And tarry for the comfort of the day.

HERMIA
 ⌜Be⌝ it so, Lysander. Find you out a bed,   45
 For I upon this bank will rest my head.

LYSANDER
 One turf shall serve as pillow for us both;
 One heart, one bed, two bosoms, and one troth.

HERMIA
 Nay, good Lysander. For my sake, my dear,
 Lie further off yet. Do not lie so near.   50

LYSANDER
 O, take the sense, sweet, of my innocence!
 Love takes the meaning in love's conference.
 I mean that my heart unto yours ⌜is⌝ knit,
 So that but one heart we can make of it;
 Two bosoms interchainèd with an oath—   55
 So then two bosoms and a single troth.
 Then by your side no bed-room me deny,
 For lying so, Hermia, I do not lie.

HERMIA
 Lysander riddles very prettily.
 Now much beshrew my manners and my pride   60
 If Hermia meant to say Lysander lied.
 But, gentle friend, for love and courtesy,
 Lie further off in human modesty.
 Such separation, as may well be said,
 Becomes a virtuous bachelor and a maid.   65
 So far be distant; and good night, sweet friend.
 Thy love ne'er alter till thy sweet life end!

LYSANDER
 "Amen, amen" to that fair prayer, say I,
 And then end life when I end loyalty!
 Here is my bed. Sleep give thee all his rest!   70

74. **approve:** demonstrate, confirm; or, test
77. **Weeds:** garments
85. **owe:** i.e., own, possess
86–87. **let love . . . eyelid:** i.e., let love so torment you that you cannot close your eyes in sleep
forbid . . . seat: i.e., banish from its place
91. **charge:** command
92. **darkling:** in the dark

Robin Goodfellow. (2.1.0 SD)
From *Robin Good-fellow, his mad prankes . . .* (1639).

58

HERMIA
With half that wish the wisher's eyes be pressed!
⌈*They sleep.*⌉

Enter ⌈*Robin.*⌉

ROBIN
Through the forest have I gone,
But Athenian found I none
On whose eyes I might approve
This flower's force in stirring love.   75
⌈*He sees Lysander.*⌉
Night and silence! Who is here?
Weeds of Athens he doth wear.
This is he my master said
Despisèd the Athenian maid.
And here the maiden, sleeping sound   80
On the dank and dirty ground.
Pretty soul, she durst not lie
Near this lack-love, this kill-courtesy.—
Churl, upon thy eyes I throw
All the power this charm doth owe.   85
⌈*He anoints Lysander's eyelids*
with the nectar.⌉
When thou wak'st, let love forbid
Sleep his seat on thy eyelid.
So, awake when I am gone,
For I must now to Oberon.   *He exits.*

Enter Demetrius and Helena, running.

HELENA
Stay, though thou kill me, sweet Demetrius.   90
DEMETRIUS
I charge thee, hence, and do not haunt me thus.
HELENA
O, wilt thou darkling leave me? Do not so.

94. **fond:** (1) foolish; (2) infatuated

95. **grace:** favor or reward for prayer

103. **as:** i.e., as if I were

104. **glass:** mirror

105. **compare with:** i.e., rival, vie with; **sphery eyne:** perhaps, eyes belonging to the celestial spheres, like stars

110. **Transparent:** (1) radiant; (2) capable of being seen through; **Nature shows art:** In making Helena's body "transparent," so that Lysander can "see her heart," Nature acts like a magician. **art:** magic, power

121. **change:** i.e., exchange

122–29. **The will . . . book:** In this speech, Lysander attributes his sudden love for Helena to his having suddenly become mature and rational. **will:** desire

DEMETRIUS
    Stay, on thy peril. I alone will go.   ⌜*Demetrius exits.*⌝
HELENA
    O, I am out of breath in this fond chase.
    The more my prayer, the lesser is my grace.   95
    Happy is Hermia, wheresoe'er she lies,
    For she hath blessèd and attractive eyes.
    How came her eyes so bright? Not with salt tears.
    If so, my eyes are oftener washed than hers.
    No, no, I am as ugly as a bear,   100
    For beasts that meet me run away for fear.
    Therefore no marvel though Demetrius
    Do as a monster fly my presence thus.
    What wicked and dissembling glass of mine
    Made me compare with Hermia's sphery eyne?   105
    But who is here? Lysander, on the ground!
    Dead or asleep? I see no blood, no wound.—
    Lysander, if you live, good sir, awake.
LYSANDER, ⌜*waking up*⌝
    And run through fire I will for thy sweet sake.
    Transparent Helena! Nature shows art,   110
    That through thy bosom makes me see thy heart.
    Where is Demetrius? O, how fit a word
    Is that vile name to perish on my sword!
HELENA
    Do not say so. Lysander, say not so.
    What though he love your Hermia? Lord, what   115
        though?
    Yet Hermia still loves you. Then be content.
LYSANDER
    Content with Hermia? No, I do repent
    The tedious minutes I with her have spent.
    Not Hermia, but Helena I love.   120
    Who will not change a raven for a dove?
    The will of man is by his reason swayed,
    And reason says you are the worthier maid.

124. **Things growing:** i.e., growing things

125. **ripe not:** i.e., did not ripen

126. **point:** i.e., the highest point; **skill:** judgment, discrimination

127. **marshal:** an officer who leads guests to their proper places

128. **o'erlook:** survey

130. **Wherefore:** why

136. **Good troth, good sooth:** i.e., in truth (mild oaths)

138. **Perforce:** of necessity

147. **of those they did deceive:** i.e., by the men who had mistakenly believed in the heresies

149. **Of:** i.e., by

Things growing are not ripe until their season;
So I, being young, till now ripe not to reason.   125
And touching now the point of human skill,
Reason becomes the marshal to my will
And leads me to your eyes, where I o'erlook
Love's stories written in love's richest book.

HELENA
Wherefore was I to this keen mockery born?   130
When at your hands did I deserve this scorn?
Is 't not enough, is 't not enough, young man,
That I did never, no, nor never can
Deserve a sweet look from Demetrius' eye,
But you must flout my insufficiency?   135
Good troth, you do me wrong, good sooth, you do,
In such disdainful manner me to woo.
But fare you well. Perforce I must confess
I thought you lord of more true gentleness.
O, that a lady of one man refused   140
Should of another therefore be abused!   *She exits.*

LYSANDER
She sees not Hermia.—Hermia, sleep thou there,
And never mayst thou come Lysander near.
For, as a surfeit of the sweetest things
The deepest loathing to the stomach brings,   145
Or as the heresies that men do leave
Are hated most of those they did deceive,
So thou, my surfeit and my heresy,
Of all be hated, but the most of me!
And, all my powers, address your love and might   150
To honor Helen and to be her knight.   *He exits.*

HERMIA, ⌜*waking up*⌝
Help me, Lysander, help me! Do thy best
To pluck this crawling serpent from my breast.
Ay me, for pity! What a dream was here!
Lysander, look how I do quake with fear.   155
Methought a serpent ate my heart away,

157. **prey:** i.e., attack
160. **an if:** i.e., if

And you sat smiling at his cruel prey.
Lysander! What, removed? Lysander, lord!
What, out of hearing? Gone? No sound, no word?
Alack, where are you? Speak, an if you hear.   160
Speak, of all loves! I swoon almost with fear.—
No? Then I well perceive you are not nigh.
Either death or you I'll find immediately.

She exits.

A
MIDSUMMER
NIGHT'S DREAM

ACT 3

3.1 The tradesmen meet in the woods to rehearse. Robin Goodfellow happens upon them and transforms Bottom's head into that of an ass. Abandoned by his terrified friends, Bottom sings. His singing awakens Titania, who, under the influence of the flower's magic, falls in love with him. She takes him away to sleep in her bower.

———

0 SD. **Clowns:** i.e., actors who play comic roles

2. **Pat:** i.e., at exactly the right time; **marvels:** i.e., marvelously

3. **plot:** piece of ground

4. **brake:** thicket; **tiring-house:** i.e., attiring house, dressing room

8. **bully:** worthy, admirable

13. **By 'r lakin:** an oath "by our Lady"; **parlous:** perilous, terrible

15. **when all is done:** i.e., after all

ΓScene 1⅂
Γ*With Titania still asleep onstage,*⅂ *enter the Clowns,*
Γ*Bottom, Quince, Snout, Starveling, Snug, and Flute.*⅂

BOTTOM   Are we all met?

QUINCE   Pat, pat. And here's a marvels convenient
place for our rehearsal. This green plot shall be
our stage, this hawthorn brake our tiring-house,
and we will do it in action as we will do it before   5
the Duke.

BOTTOM   Peter Quince?

QUINCE   What sayest thou, bully Bottom?

BOTTOM   There are things in this comedy of Pyramus
and Thisbe that will never please. First, Pyramus   10
must draw a sword to kill himself, which the ladies
cannot abide. How answer you that?

SNOUT   By 'r lakin, a parlous fear.

STARVELING   I believe we must leave the killing out,
when all is done.   15

BOTTOM   Not a whit! I have a device to make all well.
Write me a prologue, and let the prologue seem to
say we will do no harm with our swords, and that
Pyramus is not killed indeed. And, for the more
better assurance, tell them that I, Pyramus, am not   20
Pyramus, but Bottom the weaver. This will put them
out of fear.

24. **eight and six:** alternating eight- and six-syllable lines (the standard ballad meter)

39. **defect:** Bottom's error for "effect"

42–43. **it were pity of my life:** i.e., I would be risking my life

QUINCE Well, we will have such a prologue, and it shall
    be written in eight and six.
BOTTOM No, make it two more. Let it be written in   25
    eight and eight.
SNOUT Will not the ladies be afeard of the lion?
STARVELING I fear it, I promise you.
BOTTOM Masters, you ought to consider with yourself,
    to bring in (God shield us!) a lion among ladies is a   30
    most dreadful thing. For there is not a more fearful
    wildfowl than your lion living, and we ought to look
    to 't.
SNOUT Therefore another prologue must tell he is not
    a lion.   35
BOTTOM Nay, you must name his name, and half his
    face must be seen through the lion's neck, and he
    himself must speak through, saying thus, or to the
    same defect: "Ladies," or "Fair ladies, I would
    wish you," or "I would request you," or "I would   40
    entreat you not to fear, not to tremble! My life for
    yours. If you think I come hither as a lion, it were
    pity of my life. No, I am no such thing. I am a man as
    other men are." And there indeed let him name his
    name and tell them plainly he is Snug the joiner.   45
QUINCE Well, it shall be so. But there is two hard
    things: that is, to bring the moonlight into a cham-
    ber, for you know Pyramus and Thisbe meet by
    moonlight.
SNOUT Doth the moon shine that night we play our   50
    play?
BOTTOM A calendar, a calendar! Look in the almanac.
    Find out moonshine, find out moonshine.
                         ⌜*Quince takes out a book.*⌝
QUINCE Yes, it doth shine that night.
⌜BOTTOM⌝ Why, then, may you leave a casement of the   55
    great chamber window, where we play, open, and
    the moon may shine in at the casement.

58–59. bush of thorns: In legend, there is in the moon a man who carries a bundle of sticks and a lantern and who is often accompanied by his dog.

59. disfigure: Quince's mistake for "figure" (i.e., represent)

67–68. plaster . . . loam . . . roughcast: Each of these is used for plastering walls. **Plaster** is a mixture of lime, sand, and hair; **loam** is a mixture of clay, sand, and straw (it was also used for making bricks); **roughcast** is a mixture of lime and gravel.

69. thus: The actor playing Bottom usually, at this point, makes a "V" with his first two fingers.

76. hempen homespuns: i.e., country bumpkins, wearing homespun clothes woven from hemp

77. cradle: i.e., the bower where Titania is sleeping

78. toward: about to take place

QUINCE   Ay, or else one must come in with a bush of
thorns and a lantern and say he comes to disfigure
or to present the person of Moonshine. Then there   60
is another thing: we must have a wall in the great
chamber, for Pyramus and Thisbe, says the story,
did talk through the chink of a wall.

SNOUT   You can never bring in a wall. What say you,
Bottom?   65

BOTTOM   Some man or other must present Wall. And
let him have some plaster, or some loam, or some
roughcast about him to signify wall, or let him
hold his fingers thus, and through that cranny shall
Pyramus and Thisbe whisper.   70

QUINCE   If that may be, then all is well. Come, sit down,
every mother's son, and rehearse your parts. Pyramus, you begin. When you have spoken your
speech, enter into that brake, and so everyone
according to his cue.   75

Enter Robin ⌐*invisible to those onstage.*⌐

ROBIN, ⌐*aside*⌐
What hempen homespuns have we swagg'ring here
So near the cradle of the Fairy Queen?
What, a play toward? I'll be an auditor—
An actor too perhaps, if I see cause.

QUINCE   Speak, Pyramus.—Thisbe, stand forth.   80

BOTTOM, *as Pyramus*
    Thisbe, the flowers of odious savors sweet—

QUINCE   Odors, ⌐*odors!*⌐

BOTTOM, *as Pyramus*
                    . . . odors savors sweet.
    So hath thy breath, my dearest Thisbe dear.—
    But hark, a voice! Stay thou but here awhile,   85
    And by and by I will to thee appear.   *He exits.*

⌐ROBIN, *aside*⌐
A stranger Pyramus than e'er played here. ⌐*He exits.*⌐

89. **marry:** i.e., indeed

92–95. **Most . . . tire:** These lines include several words that simply fill out the six-beat doggerel lines (**brisky** [rather than "brisk"], **juvenal** [rather than "youth"], **eke** [i.e., also]) and words that seem desperate attempts to rhyme (**Jew** to rhyme with **hue, tire** to rhyme with **brier**). Part of the comedy in the "Pyramus and Thisbe" scenes turns on the very bad "poetry" of the script. **triumphant:** splendid **brier:** wild rose bush

97. **Ninus' tomb:** In Ovid's *Metamorphoses*, the lovers meet at the tomb of Ninus, legendary founder of the city of Nineveh.

99. **part:** Actors were provided with "parts" that contained cues of two or three words, as well as their own speeches. (Flute seems not to have read "cues and all," but rather to have read two of Thisbe's speeches as if they were one.)

103 SD. **with the ass-head:** i.e., wearing the "ass head" (a stage prop)

104. **were:** i.e., would be

107. **round:** roundabout way; circle dance

111. **fire:** i.e., will-o'-the-wisp

FLUTE   Must I speak now?

QUINCE   Ay, marry, must you, for you must understand
he goes but to see a noise that he heard and is to   90
come again.

FLUTE, *as Thisbe*
Most radiant Pyramus, most lily-white of hue,
Of color like the red rose on triumphant brier,
Most brisky juvenal and eke most lovely Jew,
As true as truest horse, that yet would never tire.   95
I'll meet thee, Pyramus, at Ninny's tomb.

QUINCE   "Ninus' tomb," man! Why, you must not
speak that yet. That you answer to Pyramus. You
speak all your part at once, cues and all.—Pyramus, enter. Your cue is past. It is "never tire."   100

FLUTE   O!
⌜*As Thisbe.*⌝ *As true as truest horse, that yet would never*
tire.

⌜*Enter Robin, and Bottom as Pyramus with the*
ass-head.⌝

BOTTOM, *as Pyramus*
If I were fair, ⌜*fair*⌝ *Thisbe, I were only thine.*

QUINCE   O monstrous! O strange! We are haunted. Pray,   105
masters, fly, masters! Help!
⌜*Quince, Flute, Snout, Snug, and Starveling exit.*⌝

ROBIN
I'll follow you. I'll lead you about a round,
   Through bog, through bush, through brake,
      through brier.
Sometime a horse I'll be, sometime a hound,   110
   A hog, a headless bear, sometime a fire,
And neigh, and bark, and grunt, and roar, and burn,
Like horse, hound, hog, bear, fire, at every turn.
                                          He exits.

BOTTOM   Why do they run away? This is a knavery of
them to make me afeard.   115

120–21. **translated:** transformed

127. **ouzel:** blackbird

129. **throstle:** thrush

130. **little quill:** i.e., small note (literally, a small musical pipe)

133. **plainsong cuckoo gray:** i.e., gray cuckoo, whose repetitive call is as simple as the early church music called **plainsong** (See page 80.)

134. **Whose . . . mark:** i.e., whose song many men hear and pay attention to (Because the cuckoo does not build nests but leaves its eggs for other birds to hatch and feed, its song of "cuckoo" is linked to "cuckold," a man whose wife is unfaithful and thus who might bear children fathered by other men. Its call was considered a mocking cry directed at married men.)

136. **who . . . foolish:** Proverbial: "Do not set your wit against a fool's." **set his wit:** use his intelligence to answer

137. **give . . . the lie:** accuse . . . of lying

138. **never so:** countless times (i.e., over and over)

140. **note:** song

142. **virtue's:** excellence's; **perforce:** i.e., whether I want to or not, willy-nilly; **move me:** persuade me; stir my emotions

Enter Snout.

SNOUT   O Bottom, thou art changed! What do I see on
thee?

BOTTOM   What do you see? You see an ass-head of your
own, do you?   ⌜*Snout exits.*⌝

Enter Quince.

QUINCE   Bless thee, Bottom, bless thee! Thou art trans-   120
lated!   *He exits.*

BOTTOM   I see their knavery. This is to make an ass of
me, to fright me, if they could. But I will not stir
from this place, do what they can. I will walk up
and down here, and I will sing, that they shall hear   125
I am not afraid.
⌜*He sings.*⌝ *The ouzel cock, so black of hue,*
With orange-tawny bill,
The throstle with his note so true,
The wren with little quill—   130

TITANIA, ⌜*waking up*⌝
What angel wakes me from my flow'ry bed?

BOTTOM ⌜*sings*⌝
The finch, the sparrow, and the lark,
The plainsong cuckoo gray,
Whose note full many a man doth mark
And dares not answer "nay"—   135
for, indeed, who would set his wit to so foolish a
bird? Who would give a bird the lie though he cry
"cuckoo" never so?

TITANIA
I pray thee, gentle mortal, sing again.
Mine ear is much enamored of thy note,   140
So is mine eye enthrallèd to thy shape,
And thy fair virtue's force perforce doth move me
On the first view to say, to swear, I love thee.

BOTTOM   Methinks, mistress, you should have little

146. **keep little company together:** i.e., are not good friends

148. **gleek:** make a joke

156. **common:** ordinary; **rate:** value

157. **still:** always; **doth tend upon:** serves, attends; **state:** greatness, position of power

160. **deep:** ocean

162–63. **I will purge . . . go:** i.e., I will transform you into a spirit **purge:** make pure or clean **mortal:** i.e., subject to death (It has been suggested that the medical meaning of **purge** [i.e., to cleanse the body through bleedings or laxatives] should be considered here.)

164 SD. **Peaseblossom . . . Mustardseed:** Each of these names indicates something very tiny or otherwise hard to see. **Peaseblossom:** the flower of the pea plant **Mote:** speck (Since the words *mote* and *moth* were pronounced the same way, and since the character's name is spelled "moth" in the early printings of this play, the character's name might mean, instead, a small flying insect. "Mote" is an almost-silent character, not described in the dialogue as the other fairies are. Thus editors have difficulty determining whether his/its name should, in modern spelling, be "Mote" or "Moth.") **Mustardseed:** It is from tiny mustardseeds that mustard is made.

171. **gambol:** skip, leap about; **in his eyes:** in his sight

172. **apricocks:** apricots; **dewberries:** blackberries

174. **humble-bees:** bumble bees

reason for that. And yet, to say the truth, reason   145
and love keep little company together nowadays.
The more the pity that some honest neighbors will
not make them friends. Nay, I can gleek upon
occasion.

TITANIA
Thou art as wise as thou art beautiful.   150

BOTTOM Not so neither; but if I had wit enough to get
out of this wood, I have enough to serve mine own
turn.

TITANIA
Out of this wood do not desire to go.
Thou shalt remain here whether thou wilt or no.   155
I am a spirit of no common rate.
The summer still doth tend upon my state,
And I do love thee. Therefore go with me.
I'll give thee fairies to attend on thee,
And they shall fetch thee jewels from the deep   160
And sing while thou on pressèd flowers dost sleep.
And I will purge thy mortal grossness so
That thou shalt like an airy spirit go.—
Peaseblossom, Cobweb, Mote, and Mustardseed!

Enter four Fairies: ⌜*Peaseblossom, Cobweb,*
Mote, and Mustardseed.⌝

⌜PEASEBLOSSOM⌝ Ready.   165
⌜COBWEB⌝ And I.
⌜MOTE⌝ And I.
⌜MUSTARDSEED⌝ And I.
⌜ALL⌝ Where shall we go?

TITANIA
Be kind and courteous to this gentleman.   170
Hop in his walks and gambol in his eyes;
Feed him with apricocks and dewberries,
With purple grapes, green figs, and mulberries;
The honey-bags steal from the humble-bees,

177. **have:** i.e., attend

185. **cry . . . mercy:** i.e., beg . . . pardon

189–90. **Cobweb . . . you:** Cobwebs were used to stop bleeding.

190. **honest:** honorable

192. **Squash:** an unripened pea-pod

193. **Peascod:** a ripe pea-pod

198–99. **your patience:** perhaps, referring to mustard's patience in being so often devoured; perhaps, "your Patience," as in "your Honor"

199. **ox-beef:** Mustard is often served as a condiment with beef. (Bottom is here sympathizing with Mustardseed for having lost kinsmen who have been eaten as mustard.)

207. **enforcèd chastity:** (1) chastity enforced, compelled; (2) chastity forced and destroyed, raped

A "cuckoo gray." (3.1.133)
From Konrad Gesner, . . . *Historia animalium* . . . (1585).

And for night-tapers crop their waxen thighs   175
And light them at the fiery glowworms' eyes
To have my love to bed and to arise;
And pluck the wings from painted butterflies
To fan the moonbeams from his sleeping eyes.
Nod to him, elves, and do him courtesies.   180
⌜PEASEBLOSSOM⌝   Hail, mortal!
⌜COBWEB⌝   Hail!
⌜MOTE⌝   Hail!
⌜MUSTARDSEED⌝   Hail!
BOTTOM   I cry your Worships mercy, heartily.—I be- 185
seech your Worship's name.
COBWEB   Cobweb.
BOTTOM   I shall desire you of more acquaintance, good
Master Cobweb. If I cut my finger, I shall make
bold with you.—Your name, honest gentleman?   190
PEASEBLOSSOM   Peaseblossom.
BOTTOM   I pray you, commend me to Mistress Squash,
your mother, and to Master Peascod, your father.
Good Master Peaseblossom, I shall desire you of
more acquaintance, too.—Your name, I beseech   195
you, sir?
MUSTARDSEED   Mustardseed.
BOTTOM   Good Master Mustardseed, I know your pa-
tience well. That same cowardly, giantlike ox-beef
hath devoured many a gentleman of your house. I 200
promise you, your kindred hath made my eyes
water ere now. I desire you ⌜of⌝ more acquaint-
ance, good Master Mustardseed.
TITANIA
Come, wait upon him. Lead him to my bower.
The moon, methinks, looks with a wat'ry eye,   205
And when she weeps, weeps every little flower,
Lamenting some enforcèd chastity.
Tie up my lover's tongue. Bring him silently.
                                            ⌜*They*⌝ *exit.*

3.2 Robin Goodfellow reports to Oberon about Titania and Bottom. When Demetrius enters wooing Hermia, Oberon discovers that Robin has anointed the eyes of the wrong Athenian. Oberon then orders Robin to fetch Helena while he anoints the eyes of the sleeping Demetrius. Helena enters pursued by Lysander vowing his love. Demetrius awakes, falls in love with Helena, and also begins to woo her. Helena believes both men are mocking her. When Hermia arrives and learns that Lysander has abandoned her for Helena, she threatens Helena, who thinks that Hermia is part of the conspiracy. Lysander and Demetrius prepare to duel to prove their right to Helena. At Oberon's command, Robin impersonates each of the two men in turn in order to lead the other astray until both, exhausted, fall asleep. Helena and Hermia also fall asleep. Robin applies nectar to Lysander's eyes to undo the spell that has drawn him to Helena.

———————

3. **in extremity:** to the highest degree
5. **night-rule:** perhaps, disorder (night being associated with the irrational); **haunted:** much visited
7. **close:** hidden, secluded
8. **dull:** i.e., unconscious (because asleep)
9. **patches:** simpletons; **rude:** humble; uncivilized; **mechanicals:** workers
10. **work for bread:** i.e., earn their livings; **stalls:** booths, sheds (where cobblers, butchers, etc., worked and sold their wares)
13. **barren:** dull
14. **sport:** drama, theatrical activity
15. **scene:** stage

(continued)

⌜Scene 2⌝
Enter ⌜*Oberon,*⌝ *King of Fairies.*

OBERON
　I wonder if Titania be awaked;
　Then what it was that next came in her eye,
　Which she must dote on in extremity.

　　⌜*Enter Robin Goodfellow.*⌝

　Here comes my messenger. How now, mad spirit?
　What night-rule now about this haunted grove?　　　5
ROBIN
　My mistress with a monster is in love.
　Near to her close and consecrated bower,
　While she was in her dull and sleeping hour,
　A crew of patches, rude mechanicals,
　That work for bread upon Athenian stalls,　　　10
　Were met together to rehearse a play
　Intended for great Theseus' nuptial day.
　The shallowest thick-skin of that barren sort,
　Who Pyramus presented in their sport,
　Forsook his scene and entered in a brake.　　　15
　When I did him at this advantage take,
　An ass's noll I fixèd on his head.
　Anon his Thisbe must be answerèd,
　And forth my ⌜mimic⌝ comes. When they him spy,
　As wild geese that the creeping fowler eye,　　　20
　Or russet-pated choughs, many in sort,
　Rising and cawing at the gun's report,
　Sever themselves and madly sweep the sky,
　So at his sight away his fellows fly,
　And, at our stamp, here o'er and o'er one falls.　　　25
　He "Murder" cries and help from Athens calls.
　Their sense thus weak, lost with their fears thus
　　　strong,
　Made senseless things begin to do them wrong;

17. **noll:** head
18. **Anon:** soon
19. **mimic:** i.e., comic actor
20. **fowler:** one who hunts wild birds
21. **russet-pated . . . sort:** a large flock of brownish-headed jackdaws
23. **Sever themselves:** i.e., split up
25. **at our stamp:** Robin, as described in stories and ballads, has a powerful stamp. However, since his use of "our" is puzzling, it has been suggested that "at our stamp" is a misprint for "at a stump."
31–32. **from . . . catch:** perhaps, everything snatches at cowards
34. **translated:** transformed
37. **falls out:** happens
38. **latched:** snared, caught
42. **That:** i.e., so that; **of force:** of necessity (i.e., inevitably)
43. **Stand close:** an order to step aside into hiding
50. **o'er shoes:** i.e., up to your ankles
55–57. **This whole earth . . . Antipodes:** i.e., that the solid globe could be so pierced that the moon could travel through it, bringing night to the Antipodes when it should there be noon **bored:** pierced through, drilled **Her brother's:** i.e., the sun's **Antipodes:** the region on the opposite side of the globe (See page 86.)

For briers and thorns at their apparel snatch,   30
Some sleeves, some hats, from yielders all things
    catch.
I led them on in this distracted fear
And left sweet Pyramus translated there.
When in that moment, so it came to pass,   35
Titania waked and straightway loved an ass.

OBERON
This falls out better than I could devise.
But hast thou yet latched the Athenian's eyes
With the love juice, as I did bid thee do?

ROBIN
I took him sleeping—that is finished, too—   40
And the Athenian woman by his side,
That, when he waked, of force she must be eyed.

        Enter Demetrius and Hermia.

OBERON
Stand close. This is the same Athenian.

ROBIN
This is the woman, but not this the man.
                              ⌐*They step aside.*⌐

DEMETRIUS
O, why rebuke you him that loves you so?   45
Lay breath so bitter on your bitter foe!

HERMIA
Now I but chide, but I should use thee worse,
For thou, I fear, hast given me cause to curse.
If thou hast slain Lysander in his sleep,
Being o'er shoes in blood, plunge in the deep   50
And kill me too.
The sun was not so true unto the day
As he to me. Would he have stolen away
From sleeping Hermia? I'll believe as soon
This whole earth may be bored, and that the moon   55
May through the center creep and so displease

59. **dead:** (1) deadly; (2) dull; (3) deathly pale

64. **What's this to:** i.e., what does this have to do with

71. **being awake:** i.e., if Lysander were awake

73. **worm:** serpent

75. **never adder stung:** i.e., never did adder sting

76. **misprised:** mistaken; **mood:** perhaps, anger, or grief; perhaps, state of mind

80. **An if:** i.e., if; **therefor:** for it, in exchange

A map of the globe showing the Antipodes. (3.2.57)
From Macrobius, *Insomnium Scipionis exposito* . . . (1492).

Her brother's noontide with th' Antipodes.
It cannot be but thou hast murdered him.
So should a murderer look, so dead, so grim.

DEMETRIUS
So should the murdered look, and so should I,　　60
Pierced through the heart with your stern cruelty.
Yet you, the murderer, look as bright, as clear,
As yonder Venus in her glimmering sphere.

HERMIA
What's this to my Lysander? Where is he?
Ah, good Demetrius, wilt thou give him me?　　65

DEMETRIUS
I had rather give his carcass to my hounds.

HERMIA
Out, dog! Out, cur! Thou driv'st me past the bounds
Of maiden's patience. Hast thou slain him, then?
Henceforth be never numbered among men.
O, once tell true! Tell true, even for my sake!　　70
Durst thou have looked upon him, being awake?
And hast thou killed him sleeping? O brave touch!
Could not a worm, an adder, do so much?
An adder did it, for with doubler tongue
Than thine, thou serpent, never adder stung.　　75

DEMETRIUS
You spend your passion on a misprised mood.
I am not guilty of Lysander's blood,
Nor is he dead, for aught that I can tell.

HERMIA
I pray thee, tell me then that he is well.

DEMETRIUS
An if I could, what should I get therefor?　　80

HERMIA
A privilege never to see me more.
And from thy hated presence part I ⌜so.⌝
See me no more, whether he be dead or no.
　　　　　　　　　　　　　　　She exits.

86–89. So sorrow's . . . stay: Demetrius, explaining that he will now lie down and sleep, plays with two meanings of the word **heavy** (sad; sleepy). He says that sorrow grows heavier when sleep, like a bankrupt, cannot pay its debts; he lies down to wait for sleep to make him an offer (a **tender**) and pay part of its debt.

92. Of thy misprision: from your mistake; **perforce:** necessarily

93. turned: altered; changed

94–95. Then fate . . . oath: Robin attributes his mistake to fate, claiming that for every man who is faithful a million are fickle. **holding troth:** keeping his plighted oath **confounding:** breaking

96. About the wood go: i.e., go through the forest

97. look thou: i.e., make sure you

98. fancy-sick: lovesick; **cheer:** face

99. costs . . . dear: Sighs were thought to deplete the blood. **dear:** dearly

101. against: i.e., to prepare for the time

103. Tartar's bow: an Oriental bow, more powerful than English bows (See page 92.)

106. apple: i.e., the pupil

107. his love: i.e., Helena

109. Venus: the planet Venus, known as the evening star (also named above at line 63)

DEMETRIUS
    There is no following her in this fierce vein.
    Here, therefore, for a while I will remain.   85
    So sorrow's heaviness doth heavier grow
    For debt that bankrout ⌈sleep⌉ doth sorrow owe,
    Which now in some slight measure it will pay,
    If for his tender here I make some stay.
                       ⌈*He*⌉ *lies down* ⌈*and falls asleep.*⌉
OBERON, ⌈*to Robin*⌉
    What hast thou done? Thou hast mistaken quite   90
    And laid the love juice on some true-love's sight.
    Of thy misprision must perforce ensue
    Some true-love turned, and not a false turned true.
ROBIN
    Then fate o'errules, that, one man holding troth,
    A million fail, confounding oath on oath.   95
OBERON
    About the wood go swifter than the wind,
    And Helena of Athens look thou find.
    All fancy-sick she is and pale of cheer
    With sighs of love that costs the fresh blood dear.
    By some illusion see thou bring her here.   100
    I'll charm his eyes against she do appear.
ROBIN   I go, I go, look how I go,
    Swifter than arrow from the Tartar's bow.⌈*He exits.*⌉
OBERON, ⌈*applying the nectar to Demetrius' eyes*⌉
        Flower of this purple dye,
        Hit with Cupid's archery,   105
        Sink in apple of his eye.
        When his love he doth espy,
        Let her shine as gloriously
        As the Venus of the sky.
        When thou wak'st, if she be by,   110
        Beg of her for remedy.

              Enter ⌈*Robin.*⌉

115. **fee:** reward

116. **fond pageant:** foolish spectacle or scene

121. **needs:** necessarily, inevitably; **sport alone:** an unrivaled entertainment

126. **Look when:** whenever, all the while

129. **badge of faith:** i.e., his tears

130. **advance:** display, exhibit

131. **When truth . . . fray:** Helena argues that Lysander is using the **truth** of his present vows to kill the **truth** of his vows to Hermia, thus creating a battle that is both **devilish** (in that he is breaking his oath) and **holy** (in that it is a battle between truths).

132. **give her o'er:** abandon her

133–34. **Weigh . . . weigh:** Balance your oaths to her against your oaths to me, and (1) you will weigh "nothing," because the scales will be evenly balanced; or, (2) since they are both empty, you will be weighing nothing.

ROBIN

Captain of our fairy band,
Helena is here at hand,
And the youth, mistook by me,
Pleading for a lover's fee.   115
Shall we their fond pageant see?
Lord, what fools these mortals be!

OBERON

Stand aside. The noise they make
Will cause Demetrius to awake.

ROBIN

Then will two at once woo one.   120
That must needs be sport alone.
And those things do best please me
That befall prepost'rously.
                                     ⌜*They step aside.*⌝

                Enter Lysander and Helena.

LYSANDER

Why should you think that I should woo in scorn?
  Scorn and derision never come in tears.   125
Look when I vow, I weep; and vows so born,
  In their nativity all truth appears.
How can these things in me seem scorn to you,
Bearing the badge of faith to prove them true?

HELENA

You do advance your cunning more and more.   130
  When truth kills truth, O devilish holy fray!
These vows are Hermia's. Will you give her o'er?
  Weigh oath with oath, and you will nothing
    weigh.
Your vows to her and me, put in two scales,   135
Will even weigh, and both as light as tales.

LYSANDER

I had no judgment when to her I swore.

HELENA

Nor none, in my mind, now you give her o'er.

141. **eyne:** eyes

142. **Crystal is muddy:** i.e., in comparison to her eyes

144. **Taurus:** a mountain range in Asia

147. **princess of pure white:** i.e., her hand; **seal:** i.e., guarantee, pledge

149. **set against:** attack

153. **join in souls:** perhaps, unite

156. **parts:** personal qualities

160. **trim:** fine (said sarcastically)

163–64. **extort . . . patience:** i.e., wring from a poor soul her patience, as if through torture **extort:** wring out

164. **make you sport:** i.e., entertain yourselves

A Tartar's bow. (3.2.103)
From Balthasar Küchler,
Repraesentatio der fürstlichen Auffzug (1611).

LYSANDER
Demetrius loves her, and he loves not you.
DEMETRIUS, ⌜*waking up*⌝
  O Helen, goddess, nymph, perfect, divine!   140
  To what, my love, shall I compare thine eyne?
  Crystal is muddy. O, how ripe in show
  Thy lips, those kissing cherries, tempting grow!
  That pure congealèd white, high Taurus' snow,
  Fanned with the eastern wind, turns to a crow   145
  When thou hold'st up thy hand. O, let me kiss
  This princess of pure white, this seal of bliss!
HELENA
  O spite! O hell! I see you all are bent
  To set against me for your merriment.
  If you were civil and knew courtesy,   150
  You would not do me thus much injury.
  Can you not hate me, as I know you do,
  But you must join in souls to mock me too?
  If you were men, as men you are in show,
  You would not use a gentle lady so,   155
  To vow and swear and superpraise my parts,
  When, I am sure, you hate me with your hearts.
  You both are rivals and love Hermia,
  And now both rivals to mock Helena.
  A trim exploit, a manly enterprise,   160
  To conjure tears up in a poor maid's eyes
  With your derision! None of noble sort
  Would so offend a virgin and extort
  A poor soul's patience, all to make you sport.
LYSANDER
  You are unkind, Demetrius. Be not so,   165
  For you love Hermia; this you know I know.
  And here with all goodwill, with all my heart,
  In Hermia's love I yield you up my part.
  And yours of Helena to me bequeath,
  Whom I do love and will do till my death.   170

172. **I will none:** i.e., I want none of her

174. **to her but as guest-wise sojourned:** i.e., journeyed to (or stayed with) her only as a visitor **but:** only   **sojourned:** traveled; stayed

179. **aby it dear:** pay dearly for it

181. **his:** i.e., its

183. **Wherein:** i.e., in that respect (of affecting the senses) in which

188, 189. **press:** push, urge

192. **oes and eyes of light:** i.e., stars   **oes:** round spangles

HELENA
Never did mockers waste more idle breath.
DEMETRIUS
Lysander, keep thy Hermia. I will none.
If e'er I loved her, all that love is gone.
My heart to her but as guest-wise sojourned,
And now to Helen is it home returned,   175
There to remain.
LYSANDER   Helen, it is not so.
DEMETRIUS
Disparage not the faith thou dost not know,
Lest to thy peril thou aby it dear.
Look where thy love comes. Yonder is thy dear.   180

Enter Hermia.

HERMIA, ⌜*to Lysander*⌝
Dark night, that from the eye his function takes,
The ear more quick of apprehension makes;
Wherein it doth impair the seeing sense,
It pays the hearing double recompense.
Thou art not by mine eye, Lysander, found;   185
Mine ear, I thank it, brought me to thy sound.
But why unkindly didst thou leave me so?
LYSANDER
Why should he stay whom love doth press to go?
HERMIA
What love could press Lysander from my side?
LYSANDER
Lysander's love, that would not let him bide,   190
Fair Helena, who more engilds the night
Than all yon fiery oes and eyes of light.
Why seek'st thou me? Could not this make thee
    know
The hate I bear thee made me leave thee so?   195
HERMIA
You speak not as you think. It cannot be.

199. **in spite of:** i.e., to spite

202. **bait:** harass, torment

205. **chid:** scolded

208. **artificial:** skillful

209. **needles:** pronounced "neeles"

211. **both in one key:** i.e., the two of us in perfect harmony

213. **incorporate:** united in one body

218-19. **Two . . . crest:** Helena here uses technical language of heraldry (**of the first, coats, crest**) to say again that she and Hermia, though in two bodies, once shared a single heart.

220. **rent:** rend, tear

223. **Our sex:** i.e., all females

225. **amazèd:** bewildered, dumbfounded (Many editions add the word "passionate" to this line, so that it reads "your passionate words"; the word is found in the Folio.)

HELENA
  Lo, she is one of this confederacy!
  Now I perceive they have conjoined all three
  To fashion this false sport in spite of me.—
  Injurious Hermia, most ungrateful maid,   200
  Have you conspired, have you with these contrived,
  To bait me with this foul derision?
  Is all the counsel that we two have shared,
  The sisters' vows, the hours that we have spent
  When we have chid the hasty-footed time   205
  For parting us—O, is all forgot?
  All schooldays' friendship, childhood innocence?
  We, Hermia, like two artificial gods,
  Have with our needles created both one flower,
  Both on one sampler, sitting on one cushion,   210
  Both warbling of one song, both in one key,
  As if our hands, our sides, voices, and minds
  Had been incorporate. So we grew together
  Like to a double cherry, seeming parted,
  But yet an union in partition,   215
  Two lovely berries molded on one stem;
  So with two seeming bodies but one heart,
  Two of the first, ⌜like⌝ coats in heraldry,
  Due but to one, and crownèd with one crest.
  And will you rent our ancient love asunder,   220
  To join with men in scorning your poor friend?
  It is not friendly; 'tis not maidenly.
  Our sex, as well as I, may chide you for it,
  Though I alone do feel the injury.
HERMIA
  I am amazèd at your words.   225
  I scorn you not. It seems that you scorn me.
HELENA
  Have you not set Lysander, as in scorn,
  To follow me and praise my eyes and face,
  And made your other love, Demetrius,

230. **spurn:** kick

232, 233. **Wherefore:** why

235. **tender:** offer; **forsooth:** in truth; a very mild oath

236. **setting on:** instigation

237. **in grace:** i.e., favored

242. **Persever:** persevere (accent on second syllable);   **sad:** serious, grave

243. **Make mouths upon:** i.e., make faces at

245. **carried:** managed; **chronicled:** i.e., written up in chronicles or histories

247. **argument:** subject of contention

250. **excuse:** defense

254. **she:** i.e., Hermia; **entreat:** i.e., persuade you through her pleading

Who even but now did spurn me with his foot,   230
To call me goddess, nymph, divine and rare,
Precious, celestial? Wherefore speaks he this
To her he hates? And wherefore doth Lysander
Deny your love (so rich within his soul)
And tender me, forsooth, affection,   235
But by your setting on, by your consent?
What though I be not so in grace as you,
So hung upon with love, so fortunate,
But miserable most, to love unloved?
This you should pity rather than despise.   240

HERMIA
I understand not what you mean by this.

HELENA
Ay, do. Persever, counterfeit sad looks,
Make mouths upon me when I turn my back,
Wink each at other, hold the sweet jest up.
This sport, well carried, shall be chronicled.   245
If you have any pity, grace, or manners,
You would not make me such an argument.
But fare you well. 'Tis partly my own fault,
Which death or absence soon shall remedy.

LYSANDER
Stay, gentle Helena. Hear my excuse,   250
My love, my life, my soul, fair Helena.

HELENA
O excellent!

HERMIA, ⌈to Lysander⌉
Sweet, do not scorn her so.

DEMETRIUS, ⌈to Lysander⌉
If she cannot entreat, I can compel.

LYSANDER
Thou canst compel no more than she entreat.   255
Thy threats have no more strength than her weak
    ⌈prayers.⌉—
Helen, I love thee. By my life, I do.

259. **by that:** i.e., by my life

262. **withdraw . . . prove it:** Lysander here challenges Demetrius to prove his love in a duel.

265. **Ethiop:** Like "tawny Tartar" at line 274, this seems a reference to the dark color of Hermia's hair or complexion. (An **Ethiop** was a dark-skinned African.)

266–68. **No . . . follow:** These lines are difficult as printed in the quarto. Many editors substitute the Folio's "sir" for "he'll," thus solving the problem of the shift from "he" to "you." **Take on as:** i.e., act as if

274. **Tartar:** i.e., Gypsy

277. **sooth:** truly (a very mild oath)

278. **my word with thee:** i.e., my challenge to you

279–80. **bond . . . bond:** a quibble on **bond** as a binding legal agreement and **bond** as a fetter or chain (Hermia is the **weak bond** holding Lysander.)

I swear by that which I will lose for thee,
To prove him false that says I love thee not.   260
DEMETRIUS
I say I love thee more than he can do.
LYSANDER
If thou say so, withdraw and prove it too.
DEMETRIUS
Quick, come.
HERMIA   Lysander, whereto tends all this?
                        ⌜*She takes hold of Lysander.*⌝
LYSANDER
Away, you Ethiop!   265
DEMETRIUS, ⌜*to Hermia*⌝
                No, no. He'll
Seem to break loose. ⌜*To Lysander.*⌝ Take on as you
    would follow,
But yet come not. You are a tame man, go!
LYSANDER, ⌜*to Hermia*⌝
Hang off, thou cat, thou burr! Vile thing, let loose,   270
Or I will shake thee from me like a serpent.
HERMIA
Why are you grown so rude? What change is this,
Sweet love?
LYSANDER   Thy love? Out, tawny Tartar, out!
Out, loathèd med'cine! O, hated potion, hence!   275
HERMIA
Do you not jest?
HELENA   Yes, sooth, and so do you.
LYSANDER
Demetrius, I will keep my word with thee.
DEMETRIUS
I would I had your bond. For I perceive
A weak bond holds you. I'll not trust your word.   280
LYSANDER
What? Should I hurt her, strike her, kill her dead?
Although I hate her, I'll not harm her so.

284. **what news:** i.e., what does this mean?
286. **erewhile:** a little while ago
296. **juggler:** trickster, deceiver; **cankerblossom:** i.e., cankerworm, a worm that destroys flower buds
306. **urged:** i.e., put forward as a recommendation

A cankerblossom. (3.2.296)
From John Johnstone, *Opera aliquot . . .* (1650–1662).

HERMIA

What, can you do me greater harm than hate?
Hate me? Wherefore? O me, what news, my love?
Am not I Hermia? Are not you Lysander?   285
I am as fair now as I was erewhile.
Since night you loved me; yet since night you left
    me.
Why, then, you left me—O, the gods forbid!—
In earnest, shall I say?   290

LYSANDER   Ay, by my life,
And never did desire to see thee more.
Therefore be out of hope, of question, of doubt.
Be certain, nothing truer, 'tis no jest
That I do hate thee and love Helena.   295
                        ⌜*Hermia turns him loose.*⌝

HERMIA

O me! ⌜*To Helena.*⌝ You juggler, you cankerblossom,
You thief of love! What, have you come by night
And stol'n my love's heart from him?

HELENA   Fine, i' faith.
Have you no modesty, no maiden shame,   300
No touch of bashfulness? What, will you tear
Impatient answers from my gentle tongue?
Fie, fie, you counterfeit, you puppet, you!

HERMIA

"Puppet"? Why so? Ay, that way goes the game.
Now I perceive that she hath made compare   305
Between our statures; she hath urged her height,
And with her personage, her tall personage,
Her height, forsooth, she hath prevailed with him.
And are you grown so high in his esteem
Because I am so dwarfish and so low?   310
How low am I, thou painted maypole? Speak!
How low am I? I am not yet so low
But that my nails can reach unto thine eyes.

315, 316. **curst, shrewishness:** These words (like **shrewd** at 3.2.340) were used to describe women who were considered quarrelsome, talkative, or sharp-tongued.

317. **a right maid:** i.e., a girl indeed, a real sissy

319. **something:** i.e., somewhat

328. **chid me hence:** i.e., tried to drive me away through scolding

330. **so:** i.e., if

333. **fond:** foolish; or, doting

339. **she:** i.e., Hermia; **her:** i.e., Helena's

340. **keen:** cruel, fierce; **shrewd:** i.e., shrewish

HELENA
　I pray you, though you mock me, ⌈gentlemen,⌉
　Let her not hurt me. I was never curst;　　　　　　315
　I have no gift at all in shrewishness.
　I am a right maid for my cowardice.
　Let her not strike me. You perhaps may think,
　Because she is something lower than myself,
　That I can match her.　　　　　　　　　　　　320
HERMIA　　　　　　　　"Lower"? Hark, again!
HELENA
　Good Hermia, do not be so bitter with me.
　I evermore did love you, Hermia,
　Did ever keep your counsels, never wronged you—
　Save that, in love unto Demetrius,　　　　　　325
　I told him of your stealth unto this wood.
　He followed you; for love, I followed him.
　But he hath chid me hence and threatened me
　To strike me, spurn me, nay, to kill me too.
　And now, so you will let me quiet go,　　　　　330
　To Athens will I bear my folly back
　And follow you no further. Let me go.
　You see how simple and how fond I am.
HERMIA
　Why, get you gone. Who is 't that hinders you?
HELENA
　A foolish heart that I leave here behind.　　　335
HERMIA
　What, with Lysander?
HELENA　　　　　　　　　With Demetrius.
LYSANDER
　Be not afraid. She shall not harm thee, Helena.
DEMETRIUS
　No, sir, she shall not, though you take her part.
HELENA
　O, when she is angry, she is keen and shrewd.　　340
　She was a vixen when she went to school,
　And though she be but little, she is fierce.

344. **suffer:** allow

345. **come to her:** i.e., get at her

347. **minimus:** i.e., tiniest of creatures; **knotgrass:** a weed that was thought to stunt growth

354. **aby:** pay for

356–57. **whose right . . . is most in:** i.e., who has the most right to

359. **coil:** turmoil; **is long of:** i.e., is because of

365. **amazed:** astounded (as if lost in a maze)

366. **Still thou:** i.e., you always, you continue to

368. **shadows:** illusions, spirits; also, darkness

HERMIA
  "Little" again? Nothing ⌜but⌝ "low" and "little"?
  Why will you suffer her to flout me thus?
  Let me come to her.   345
LYSANDER   Get you gone, you dwarf,
  You minimus of hind'ring knotgrass made,
  You bead, you acorn—
DEMETRIUS   You are too officious
  In her behalf that scorns your services.   350
  Let her alone. Speak not of Helena.
  Take not her part. For if thou dost intend
  Never so little show of love to her,
  Thou shalt aby it.
LYSANDER   Now she holds me not.   355
  Now follow, if thou dar'st, to try whose right,
  Of thine or mine, is most in Helena.
DEMETRIUS
  "Follow"? Nay, I'll go with thee, cheek by jowl.
                    ⌜*Demetrius and Lysander exit.*⌝
HERMIA
  You, mistress, all this coil is long of you.
                              ⌜*Helena retreats.*⌝
  Nay, go not back.   360
HELENA   I will not trust you, I,
  Nor longer stay in your curst company.
  Your hands than mine are quicker for a fray.
  My legs are longer though, to run away. ⌜*She exits.*⌝
HERMIA
  I am amazed and know not what to say. ⌜*She exits.*⌝ 365
OBERON, ⌜*to Robin*⌝
  This is thy negligence. Still thou mistak'st,
  Or else committ'st thy knaveries willfully.
ROBIN
  Believe me, king of shadows, I mistook.
  Did not you tell me I should know the man
  By the Athenian garments he had on?   370

373. **it so did sort:** i.e., that it happened this way

374. **As:** since

376. **Hie:** hurry

377. **welkin:** sky; **anon:** immediately

378. **Acheron:** i.e., hell (literally, one of the four rivers of the classical underworld, Hades)

380. **As one come:** i.e., so that one comes

384. **from:** i.e., away from

386. **batty:** batlike

387. **herb:** plant, flower

388. **liquor:** juice; **virtuous property:** potent power

389. **his might:** i.e., its strength

390. **wonted sight:** i.e., usual (normal) vision

392. **fruitless:** idle, empty

394. **With league . . . end:** i.e., united in a compact that will last until death   **date:** duration, term

397. **charmèd:** bewitched

400. **night's swift dragons:** Night is here presented as driving across the sky in a chariot drawn by dragons.

401. **Aurora's harbinger:** i.e., Venus, the morning star, announcing the approach of dawn (**Aurora**)

And so far blameless proves my enterprise
That I have 'nointed an Athenian's eyes;
And so far am I glad it so did sort,
As this their jangling I esteem a sport.

OBERON
Thou seest these lovers seek a place to fight.   375
Hie, therefore, Robin, overcast the night;
The starry welkin cover thou anon
With drooping fog as black as Acheron,
And lead these testy rivals so astray
As one come not within another's way.   380
Like to Lysander sometime frame thy tongue;
Then stir Demetrius up with bitter wrong.
And sometime rail thou like Demetrius.
And from each other look thou lead them thus,
Till o'er their brows death-counterfeiting sleep   385
With leaden legs and batty wings doth creep.
Then crush this herb into Lysander's eye,
                    ⌜*He gives the flower to Robin.*⌝
Whose liquor hath this virtuous property,
To take from thence all error with his might
And make his eyeballs roll with wonted sight.   390
When they next wake, all this derision
Shall seem a dream and fruitless vision.
And back to Athens shall the lovers wend,
With league whose date till death shall never end.
Whiles I in this affair do thee employ,   395
I'll to my queen and beg her Indian boy;
And then I will her charmèd eye release
From monster's view, and all things shall be peace.

ROBIN
My fairy lord, this must be done with haste,
For night's swift dragons cut the clouds full fast,   400
And yonder shines Aurora's harbinger,
At whose approach, ghosts wand'ring here and
    there

405. **in crossways . . . burial:** i.e., those not buried in sacred ground **crossways:** i.e., crossroads, where the bodies of suicides were buried

409. **for aye:** i.e., forever

411–15. **I . . . streams:** i.e., I do not have to flee the daylight (as do the ghosts of the damned) **the Morning's love:** perhaps, Aurora herself **the eastern gate:** i.e., where the sun rises **Neptune:** i.e., the ocean

421. **Goblin:** i.e., hobgoblin (another name for Robin Goodfellow)

424. **drawn:** i.e., with my sword out

425. **straight:** straightway, immediately

427. **plainer:** flatter, more level

Neptune, god of the sea. (2.1.130)
From Johann Basilius Herold, *Heydenweldt* . . . (1554).

Troop home to churchyards. Damnèd spirits all,
That in crossways and floods have burial,   405
Already to their wormy beds are gone.
For fear lest day should look their shames upon,
They willfully themselves exile from light
And must for aye consort with black-browed night.
OBERON
But we are spirits of another sort.   410
I with the Morning's love have oft made sport
And, like a forester, the groves may tread
Even till the eastern gate, all fiery red,
Opening on Neptune with fair blessèd beams,
Turns into yellow gold his salt-green streams.   415
But notwithstanding, haste! Make no delay.
We may effect this business yet ere day.   ⌜*He exits.*⌝
ROBIN
              Up and down, up and down,
              I will lead them up and down.
              I am feared in field and town.   420
              Goblin, lead them up and down.
Here comes one.

Enter Lysander.

LYSANDER
Where art thou, proud Demetrius? Speak thou now.
ROBIN, ⌜*in Demetrius' voice*⌝
Here, villain, drawn and ready. Where art thou?
LYSANDER   I will be with thee straight.   425
ROBIN, ⌜*in Demetrius' voice*⌝   Follow me, then, to
      plainer ground.   ⌜*Lysander exits.*⌝

Enter Demetrius.

DEMETRIUS   Lysander, speak again.
Thou runaway, thou coward, art thou fled?
Speak! In some bush? Where dost thou hide thy   430
      head?

434. **recreant:** coward

436. **rod:** a stick used to whip a child; **defiled:** i.e., because Demetrius is such a coward, it would be shameful to fight him like a man

439. **try no manhood:** i.e., have no test of our courage

440. **still:** continually

444. **That:** i.e., so that; **in:** i.e., into a

449. **Abide me:** i.e., wait for me; **wot:** know

454–55. **buy this dear:** i.e., pay dearly for this

ROBIN, ⌜*in Lysander's voice*⌝
  Thou coward, art thou bragging to the stars,
  Telling the bushes that thou look'st for wars,
  And wilt not come? Come, recreant! Come, thou
    child!   435
  I'll whip thee with a rod. He is defiled
  That draws a sword on thee.
DEMETRIUS   Yea, art thou there?
ROBIN, ⌜*in Lysander's voice*⌝
  Follow my voice. We'll try no manhood here.
                           ⌜*They exit.*⌝

       ⌜*Enter Lysander.*⌝

LYSANDER
  He goes before me and still dares me on.   440
  When I come where he calls, then he is gone.
  The villain is much lighter-heeled than I.
  I followed fast, but faster he did fly,
  That fallen am I in dark uneven way,
  And here will rest me. Come, thou gentle day,   445
  For if but once thou show me thy gray light,
  I'll find Demetrius and revenge this spite.
             ⌜*He lies down and sleeps.*⌝

     ⌜*Enter*⌝ *Robin and Demetrius.*

ROBIN, ⌜*in Lysander's voice*⌝
  Ho, ho, ho! Coward, why com'st thou not?
DEMETRIUS
  Abide me, if thou dar'st, for well I wot
  Thou runn'st before me, shifting every place,   450
  And dar'st not stand nor look me in the face.
  Where art thou now?
ROBIN, ⌜*in Lysander's voice*⌝
                  Come hither. I am here.
DEMETRIUS
  Nay, then, thou mock'st me. Thou shalt buy this
    dear   455

458. **this cold bed:** i.e., the ground
459. **By day's approach:** i.e., as soon as day breaks
461. **Abate:** cut short
468. **curst:** angry
476. **mean:** i.e., intend to have

"Winged Cupid." (1.1.241)
From Henry Peacham, *Minerua Britanna* (1612).

If ever I thy face by daylight see.
Now go thy way. Faintness constraineth me
To measure out my length on this cold bed.
By day's approach look to be visited.

⌜*He lies down and sleeps.*⌝

Enter Helena.

HELENA
O weary night, O long and tedious night,   460
    Abate thy hours! Shine, comforts, from the east,
That I may back to Athens by daylight
    From these that my poor company detest.
And sleep, that sometimes shuts up sorrow's eye,
Steal me awhile from mine own company.   465

⌜*She lies down and*⌝ *sleeps.*

ROBIN
            Yet but three? Come one more.
            Two of both kinds makes up four.
            Here she comes, curst and sad.
            Cupid is a knavish lad
            Thus to make poor females mad.   470

⌜*Enter Hermia.*⌝

HERMIA
Never so weary, never so in woe,
    Bedabbled with the dew and torn with briers,
I can no further crawl, no further go.
    My legs can keep no pace with my desires.
Here will I rest me till the break of day.   475
Heavens shield Lysander if they mean a fray!

⌜*She lies down and sleeps.*⌝

ROBIN
            On the ground
            Sleep sound.
            I'll apply
            ⌜To⌝ your eye,   480
        Gentle lover, remedy.

⌐*Robin applies the nectar*
to Lysander's eyes.⌐

When thou wak'st,
Thou tak'st
True delight
In the sight   485
Of thy former lady's eye.
And the country proverb known,
That every man should take his own,
In your waking shall be shown.
    Jack shall have Jill;   490
    Naught shall go ill;
The man shall have his mare again, and all shall be
well.

⌐*He exits.*⌐

A MIDSUMMER NIGHT'S DREAM

ACT 4

4.1 Titania and her attendants pamper Bottom, who falls asleep with her. Oberon, watching them, tells Robin that Titania has given him the Indian boy and thus they can now remove the spells from Titania and Bottom. Reunited, Titania and Oberon use music to charm Bottom and the four lovers into a deep sleep, and then exit.

Theseus and Hippolyta, accompanied by Egeus and others, have come to the woods to celebrate May Day. They discover the four lovers asleep and wake them. Lysander now loves Hermia again, and Demetrius loves Helena. When Lysander reveals how he and Hermia fled Athens, Egeus begs Theseus to punish him. But when Demetrius announces that he now loves Helena, Theseus overrides Egeus and decrees that Lysander will marry Hermia and Demetrius Helena when Theseus himself weds Hippolyta. As the lovers depart for Athens, Bottom awakes and attempts to recall his night's experience, which seems to him now a dream.

---

2. **amiable:** charming, lovable; **coy:** caress
16. **overflown with:** submerged in

⌜ACT 4⌝

⌜Scene 1⌝
⌜*With the four lovers still asleep onstage,*⌝ *enter*
⌜*Titania,*⌝ *Queen of Fairies, and* ⌜*Bottom*⌝ *and Fairies,*
and ⌜*Oberon,*⌝ *the King, behind them* ⌜*unseen by those*
onstage.⌝

TITANIA
Come, sit thee down upon this flow'ry bed,
    While I thy amiable cheeks do coy,
And stick muskroses in thy sleek smooth head,
    And kiss thy fair large ears, my gentle joy.

BOTTOM Where's Peaseblossom?   5

PEASEBLOSSOM Ready.

BOTTOM Scratch my head, Peaseblossom. Where's
    Monsieur Cobweb?

COBWEB Ready.

BOTTOM Monsieur Cobweb, good monsieur, get you   10
    your weapons in your hand and kill me a red-hipped
    humble-bee on the top of a thistle, and, good
    monsieur, bring me the honey-bag. Do not fret
    yourself too much in the action, monsieur, and,
    good monsieur, have a care the honey-bag break   15
    not; I would be loath to have you overflown with a
    honey-bag, signior. ⌜*Cobweb exits.*⌝ Where's Mon-
    sieur Mustardseed?

MUSTARDSEED Ready.

20. **neaf:** fist
21. **leave your courtesy:** i.e., perhaps, stop bowing
23–24. **Cavalery:** i.e., Cavalier
24. **Cobweb:** Cobweb has been sent off already, and so this reference is considered an error by many editors. Some suggest "Peaseblossom" should be substituted for "Cobweb," but it is impossible to know how exactly to correct the "error."
25. **marvels:** i.e., marvelously
30. **the tongs and the bones:** instruments used in burlesque or rustic music (**Tongs** were played by hitting pieces of metal, like a modern triangle. **Bones** were pieces of bone clicked together.)
32. **provender:** hay, food for cattle
34. **bottle:** bundle
35. **fellow:** equal
40. **exposition of:** Bottom's error for "disposition to"
42. **all ways:** i.e., in every direction

Woodbine. (4.1.43)
From John Gerard, *The herball or generall historie of plantes* (1597).

BOTTOM   Give me your neaf, Monsieur Mustardseed.   20
Pray you, leave your courtesy, good monsieur.
MUSTARDSEED   What's your will?
BOTTOM   Nothing, good monsieur, but to help Cava-
lery Cobweb to scratch. I must to the barber's,
monsieur, for methinks I am marvels hairy about   25
the face. And I am such a tender ass, if my hair do
but tickle me, I must scratch.
TITANIA
What, wilt thou hear some music, my sweet love?
BOTTOM   I have a reasonable good ear in music. Let's
have the tongs and the bones.   30
TITANIA
Or say, sweet love, what thou desirest to eat.
BOTTOM   Truly, a peck of provender. I could munch
your good dry oats. Methinks I have a great desire
to a bottle of hay. Good hay, sweet hay, hath no
fellow.   35
TITANIA
I have a venturous fairy that shall seek
The squirrel's hoard and fetch thee new nuts.
BOTTOM   I had rather have a handful or two of dried
peas. But, I pray you, let none of your people stir
me; I have an exposition of sleep come upon me.   40
TITANIA
Sleep thou, and I will wind thee in my arms.—
Fairies, begone, and be all ways away.
⌜*Fairies exit.*⌝
So doth the woodbine the sweet honeysuckle
Gently entwist; the female ivy so
Enrings the barky fingers of the elm.   45
O, how I love thee! How I dote on thee!
⌜*Bottom and Titania sleep.*⌝

Enter Robin Goodfellow.

OBERON
Welcome, good Robin. Seest thou this sweet sight?

48. **dotage:** infatuation
54. **sometime:** formerly
55. **orient:** bright, lustrous
56. **flouriets:** i.e., little flowers
61. **straight:** straightway, immediately
67. **other:** i.e., others
68. **May:** i.e., they may; **repair:** go, travel
69. **accidents:** incidents, events
72. **wast wont to:** i.e., used to
74–75. **Dian's bud . . . power:** Oberon earlier explains (at 2.1.191 and 3.2.387–92) that he has in his possession a second flower that can undo the effect of the flower he calls "love-in-idleness." Here, as he applies the juice to Titania's eyes, he links the curative flower to Diana (**Dian's bud**), the goddess of chastity, and love-in-idleness to Cupid, god of love.
81. **visage:** appearance, face

Her dotage now I do begin to pity.
For, meeting her of late behind the wood,
Seeking sweet favors for this hateful fool,   50
I did upbraid her and fall out with her.
For she his hairy temples then had rounded
With coronet of fresh and fragrant flowers;
And that same dew, which sometime on the buds
Was wont to swell like round and orient pearls,   55
Stood now within the pretty flouriets' eyes,
Like tears that did their own disgrace bewail.
When I had at my pleasure taunted her,
And she in mild terms begged my patience,
I then did ask of her her changeling child,   60
Which straight she gave me, and her fairy sent
To bear him to my bower in Fairyland.
And now I have the boy, I will undo
This hateful imperfection of her eyes.
And, gentle Puck, take this transformèd scalp   65
From off the head of this Athenian swain,
That he, awaking when the other do,
May all to Athens back again repair
And think no more of this night's accidents
But as the fierce vexation of a dream.   70
But first I will release the Fairy Queen.
                    ⌜*He applies the nectar to her eyes.*⌝
          Be as thou wast wont to be.
          See as thou wast wont to see.
          Dian's bud o'er Cupid's flower
          Hath such force and blessèd power.   75
Now, my Titania, wake you, my sweet queen.
TITANIA, ⌜*waking*⌝
     My Oberon, what visions have I seen!
     Methought I was enamored of an ass.
OBERON
     There lies your love.
TITANIA   How came these things to pass?   80
     O, how mine eyes do loathe his visage now!

84. **these five:** i.e., Bottom and the four lovers
92. **solemnly:** ceremoniously
93. **triumphantly:** festively
97. **attend and mark:** i.e., pay attention, notice
99. **sad:** serious
106 SD. **Wind horn:** i.e., one or more hunting horns are blown

OBERON
    Silence awhile.—Robin, take off this head.—
    Titania, music call; and strike more dead
    Than common sleep of all these ⌜five⌝ the sense.

TITANIA
    Music, ho, music such as charmeth sleep!   85

ROBIN, ⌜*removing the ass-head from Bottom*⌝
    Now, when thou wak'st, with thine own fool's eyes
      peep.

OBERON
    Sound music.   ⌜*Music.*⌝
                  Come, my queen, take hands with me,
    And rock the ground whereon these sleepers be.   90
                      ⌜*Titania and Oberon dance.*⌝
    Now thou and I are new in amity,
    And will tomorrow midnight solemnly
    Dance in Duke Theseus' house triumphantly,
    And bless it to all fair prosperity.
    There shall the pairs of faithful lovers be   95
    Wedded, with Theseus, all in jollity.

ROBIN
            Fairy king, attend and mark.
            I do hear the morning lark.

OBERON
            Then, my queen, in silence sad
            Trip we after night's shade.   100
            We the globe can compass soon,
            Swifter than the wand'ring moon.

TITANIA
            Come, my lord, and in our flight
            Tell me how it came this night
            That I sleeping here was found   105
            With these mortals on the ground.
                ⌜*Oberon, Robin, and Titania*⌝ *exit.*

Wind horn. Enter Theseus and all his train,
        ⌜*Hippolyta, Egeus.*⌝

107. **Forester:** the official in charge of the forest land and responsible for the wild animals of the forest

108. **our observation:** i.e., our observance of May Day rites

109. **since . . . day:** i.e., since it is still early **vaward:** vanguard

110. **music of my hounds:** The cry of a pack of hounds in pursuit of hunted animals was compared to orchestral or vocal music, and its sound was much prized. At line 127, Theseus suggests that his hounds' music is more important to him than their speed.

111. **Uncouple:** i.e., unleash the hounds

114–15. **mark . . . conjunction:** i.e., listen to the sound created by the coming together of the cry of the hounds and its echo from the mountains

116. **Hercules:** a hero in Greek and Roman mythology; **Cadmus:** legendary founder of the city of Thebes

117. **bayed:** i.e., brought to bay

118. **hounds of Sparta:** Spartan hounds, celebrated for their hunting abilities

119. **chiding:** i.e., barking

124. **So:** i.e., like those of Sparta; **flewed:** with large folds of flesh about the mouth; **sanded:** i.e., sandy-colored

126. **dewlapped:** i.e., with folds of skin under their necks

127–28. **matched . . . each:** i.e., their cry was like a set of bells, each voice chiming in tune with the others **Each under each:** i.e., like notes on a scale

128. **cry:** pack; **tunable:** i.e., tuneful

131. **soft:** i.e., stop a minute

136. **of:** i.e., at

THESEUS
    Go, one of you, find out the Forester.
    For now our observation is performed,
    And, since we have the vaward of the day,
    My love shall hear the music of my hounds.   110
    Uncouple in the western valley; let them go.
    Dispatch, I say, and find the Forester.
                                ⌜*A Servant exits.*⌝
    We will, fair queen, up to the mountain's top
    And mark the musical confusion
    Of hounds and echo in conjunction.   115
HIPPOLYTA
    I was with Hercules and Cadmus once,
    When in a wood of Crete they bayed the bear
    With hounds of Sparta. Never did I hear
    Such gallant chiding, for, besides the groves,
    The skies, the fountains, every region near   120
    ⌜Seemed⌝ all one mutual cry. I never heard
    So musical a discord, such sweet thunder.
THESEUS
    My hounds are bred out of the Spartan kind,
    So flewed, so sanded; and their heads are hung
    With ears that sweep away the morning dew;   125
    Crook-kneed, and dewlapped like Thessalian bulls;
    Slow in pursuit, but matched in mouth like bells,
    Each under each. A cry more tunable
    Was never holloed to, nor cheered with horn,
    In Crete, in Sparta, nor in Thessaly.   130
    Judge when you hear.—But soft! What nymphs are
        these?
EGEUS
    My lord, this ⌜is⌝ my daughter here asleep,
    And this Lysander; this Demetrius is,
    This Helena, old Nedar's Helena.   135
    I wonder of their being here together.

137–38. **observe / The rite of May:** i.e., celebrate May Day

139. **grace:** honor; **solemnity:** observance (i.e., of May Day rites)

144. **Saint Valentine:** i.e., Valentine's Day (when birds proverbially chose their mates)

150. **jealousy:** suspicion, mistrust

152. **amazèdly:** i.e., in a state of bewilderment (as if lost in a maze)

155. **truly . . . speak:** i.e., I wish to speak the truth

159. **Without:** outside of, beyond

A hound. (4.1.118)
From George Turberville, *The noble arte of venerie or hunting* (1611).

THESEUS
  No doubt they rose up early to observe
  The rite of May, and hearing our intent,
  Came here in grace of our solemnity.
  But speak, Egeus. Is not this the day   140
  That Hermia should give answer of her choice?
EGEUS   It is, my lord.
THESEUS
  Go, bid the huntsmen wake them with their horns. ⌐
                           ⌐*A Servant exits.*⌐
      Shout within. Wind horns. They all start up.
THESEUS
  Good morrow, friends. Saint Valentine is past.
  Begin these woodbirds but to couple now?   145
   ⌐*Demetrius, Helena, Hermia, and Lysander kneel.*⌐
LYSANDER
  Pardon, my lord.
THESEUS   I pray you all, stand up.
                         ⌐*They rise.*⌐
  I know you two are rival enemies.
  How comes this gentle concord in the world,
  That hatred is so far from jealousy   150
  To sleep by hate and fear no enmity?
LYSANDER
  My lord, I shall reply amazèdly,
  Half sleep, half waking. But as yet, I swear,
  I cannot truly say how I came here.
  But, as I think—for truly would I speak,   155
  And now I do bethink me, so it is:
  I came with Hermia hither. Our intent
  Was to be gone from Athens, where we might,
  Without the peril of the Athenian law—
EGEUS
  Enough, enough!—My lord, you have enough.   160
  I beg the law, the law, upon his head.
  They would have stol'n away.—They would,
    Demetrius,

168. **hither:** i.e., to come here
169. **hither:** here
170. **in fancy:** i.e., drawn by her love
171. **wot:** know
174. **idle gaud:** worthless trinket
176. **virtue:** power
180. **like a sickness:** i.e., like one who is sick
186. **overbear:** i.e., overrule
189. **for:** i.e., because; **something:** i.e., somewhat
192. **in great solemnity:** i.e., with great ceremony

A mermaid. (2.1.155)
From August Casimir Redel,
Apophtegmata symbolica . . . (n.d.).

Thereby to have defeated you and me:
You of your wife and me of my consent,   165
Of my consent that she should be your wife.

DEMETRIUS
My lord, fair Helen told me of their stealth,
Of this their purpose hither to this wood,
And I in fury hither followed them,
Fair Helena in fancy following me.   170
But, my good lord, I wot not by what power
(But by some power it is) my love to Hermia,
Melted as the snow, seems to me now
As the remembrance of an idle gaud
Which in my childhood I did dote upon,   175
And all the faith, the virtue of my heart,
The object and the pleasure of mine eye,
Is only Helena. To her, my lord,
Was I betrothed ere I ⌈saw⌉ Hermia.
But like a sickness did I loathe this food.   180
But, as in health, come to my natural taste,
Now I do wish it, love it, long for it,
And will forevermore be true to it.

THESEUS
Fair lovers, you are fortunately met.
Of this discourse we more will hear anon.—   185
Egeus, I will overbear your will,
For in the temple by and by, with us,
These couples shall eternally be knit.—
And, for the morning now is something worn,
Our purposed hunting shall be set aside.   190
Away with us to Athens. Three and three,
We'll hold a feast in great solemnity.
Come, Hippolyta.

⌈*Theseus and his train,*
including Hippolyta and Egeus, exit.⌉

DEMETRIUS
These things seem small and undistinguishable,
Like far-off mountains turnèd into clouds.   195

196. **parted:** divided (i.e., out of focus)

199–200. **like a jewel . . . own:** i.e., as if I had found a jewel whom someone else might claim

211. **My next:** i.e., my next line

212. **Hey-ho!:** This may signal either a call or a big yawn.

213. **God's:** i.e., perhaps, may God save

216. **go about:** i.e., try

219. **patched:** i.e., dressed in motley, such as a professional fool would wear

220–24. **The eye . . . dream was:** This seems to be Bottom's confused memory of 1 Corinthians 2.9, where St. Paul writes: "The eye hath not seen, and the ear hath not heard, neither have entered into the heart of man, the things which God hath prepared for them that love him" (as translated in the Bishops' Bible [1568]).

225–26. **because it hath no bottom:** St. Paul's letter to the Corinthians continues (1 Corinthians 2.10): ". . . the spirit searcheth all things, yea the deep things of God," words that again may be confusingly echoed in Bottom's reflection on the bottomlessness of his vision.

HERMIA
  Methinks I see these things with parted eye,
  When everything seems double.
HELENA   So methinks.
  And I have found Demetrius like a jewel,
  Mine own and not mine own.   200
DEMETRIUS   Are you sure
  That we are awake? It seems to me
  That yet we sleep, we dream. Do not you think
  The Duke was here and bid us follow him?
HERMIA
  Yea, and my father.   205
HELENA   And Hippolyta.
LYSANDER
  And he did bid us follow to the temple.
DEMETRIUS
  Why, then, we are awake. Let's follow him,
  And by the way let ⌜us⌝ recount our dreams.
                              ⌜*Lovers exit.*⌝
BOTTOM, ⌜*waking up*⌝ When my cue comes, call me,   210
  and I will answer. My next is "Most fair Pyramus."
  Hey-ho! Peter Quince! Flute the bellows-mender!
  Snout the tinker! Starveling! God's my life! Stolen
  hence and left me asleep! I have had a most rare
  vision. I have had a dream past the wit of man to say   215
  what dream it was. Man is but an ass if he go about
  ⌜to⌝ expound this dream. Methought I was—there
  is no man can tell what. Methought I was and
  methought I had—but man is but ⌜a patched⌝ fool if
  he will offer to say what methought I had. The eye of   220
  man hath not heard, the ear of man hath not seen,
  man's hand is not able to taste, his tongue to
  conceive, nor his heart to report what my dream
  was. I will get Peter Quince to write a ballad of this
  dream. It shall be called "Bottom's Dream" be-   225
  cause it hath no bottom; and I will sing it in the

227–29. a play . . . her death: It has been suggested that the vagueness here about "a play" and "her death" are signs that Bottom is still half asleep.

4.2 The tradesmen regret, for their own sakes and for Bottom's, the loss of their opportunity to perform the play, since Bottom is irreplaceable. Bottom arrives and announces that their play has been chosen by Theseus for performance that night.

---

3. **Out of doubt:** i.e., surely
4. **transported:** i.e., transformed; carried away
5–6. **It goes . . . doth it?:** i.e., it won't go on, will it?
8. **discharge:** i.e., play, perform
11. **person:** personage, appearance
14. **thing of naught:** an evil thing
17–18. **we . . . men:** i.e., our fortunes would have been made
19–20. **six pence . . . life:** Such a daily pension would have been very grand.
21. **An:** if

latter end of a play, before the Duke. Peradventure,
to make it the more gracious, I shall sing it at her
death.

⌜*He exits.*⌝

⌜Scene 2⌝
Enter Quince, Flute, ⌜*Snout, and Starveling.*⌝

QUINCE   Have you sent to Bottom's house? Is he come
home yet?
⌜STARVELING⌝   He cannot be heard of. Out of doubt he
is transported.
FLUTE   If he come not, then the play is marred. It goes   5
not forward, doth it?
QUINCE   It is not possible. You have not a man in all
Athens able to discharge Pyramus but he.
FLUTE   No, he hath simply the best wit of any handi-
craftman in Athens.   10
QUINCE   Yea, and the best person too, and he is a very
paramour for a sweet voice.
FLUTE   You must say "paragon." A "paramour" is (God
bless us) a thing of naught.

Enter Snug the joiner.

SNUG   Masters, the Duke is coming from the temple,   15
and there is two or three lords and ladies more
married. If our sport had gone forward, we had all
been made men.
FLUTE   O, sweet bully Bottom! Thus hath he lost six
pence a day during his life. He could not have   20
'scaped six pence a day. An the Duke had not given
him six pence a day for playing Pyramus, I'll be
hanged. He would have deserved it. Six pence a day
in Pyramus, or nothing!

Enter Bottom.

26. **hearts:** hearties, good fellows

31–32. **right . . . fell out:** just . . . happened

34. **of me:** i.e., from me

36. **strings to your beards:** i.e., strings to tie on your false beards

36–37. **ribbons to your pumps:** i.e., ribbons to decorate your fancy shoes

37. **presently:** right away

39. **preferred:** recommended

BOTTOM   Where are these lads? Where are these   25
hearts?

QUINCE   Bottom! O most courageous day! O most happy hour!

BOTTOM   Masters, I am to discourse wonders. But ask
me not what; for, if I tell you, I am not true   30
Athenian. I will tell you everything right as it fell
out.

QUINCE   Let us hear, sweet Bottom.

BOTTOM   Not a word of me. All that I will tell you is that
the Duke hath dined. Get your apparel together,   35
good strings to your beards, new ribbons to your
pumps. Meet presently at the palace. Every man
look o'er his part. For the short and the long is, our
play is preferred. In any case, let Thisbe have clean
linen, and let not him that plays the lion pare his   40
nails, for they shall hang out for the lion's claws.
And, most dear actors, eat no onions nor garlic, for
we are to utter sweet breath, and I do not doubt but
to hear them say it is a sweet comedy. No more
words. Away! Go, away!   45

⌜*They exit.*⌝

A
MIDSUMMER
NIGHT'S DREAM

ACT 5

5.1 Theseus dismisses as imaginary the lovers' account of their night's experience, and then chooses "Pyramus and Thisbe" for the night's entertainment. The play is so ridiculous and the performance so bad that the courtly audience find pleasure in mocking them. When the play is over and the newly married couples have retired to bed, the fairies enter, led by Titania and Oberon, to bless the three marriages. Robin Goodfellow asks the audience to think of the play as if it were a dream.

---

1. **that:** i.e., that which, what
2. **may:** i.e., can
3. **antique fables:** (1) old stories; (2) fantastic tales; **fairy toys:** i.e., foolish tales (**toys**) about fairies
5. **shaping fantasies:** i.e., creative imaginations; **apprehend:** conceive, imagine
6. **comprehends:** grasps, understands
8. **of imagination all compact:** i.e., made up entirely of imagination
10. **all as frantic:** i.e., just as insane
11. **Helen's beauty:** i.e., the beauty of the legendary Helen of Troy; **a brow of Egypt:** i.e., a Gypsy-like face (another allusion to the supposed unattractiveness of women with darker coloring)

⌜ACT 5⌝

⌜Scene 1⌝

Enter Theseus, Hippolyta, and Philostrate, ⌜Lords, and Attendants.⌝

HIPPOLYTA
'Tis strange, my Theseus, that these lovers speak of.
THESEUS
More strange than true. I never may believe
These antique fables, nor these fairy toys.
Lovers and madmen have such seething brains,
Such shaping fantasies, that apprehend   5
More than cool reason ever comprehends.
The lunatic, the lover, and the poet
Are of imagination all compact.
One sees more devils than vast hell can hold:
That is the madman. The lover, all as frantic,   10
Sees Helen's beauty in a brow of Egypt.
The poet's eye, in a fine frenzy rolling,
Doth glance from heaven to earth, from earth to
    heaven,
And as imagination bodies forth   15
The forms of things unknown, the poet's pen
Turns them to shapes and gives to airy nothing
A local habitation and a name.
Such tricks hath strong imagination
That, if it would but apprehend some joy,   20

21. **comprehends:** includes (as a part of its conception of the joy); **some bringer of:** i.e., someone or something that brings

25. **all . . . together:** i.e., their minds all suffering the same transformation

26. **More witnesseth than fancy's images:** i.e., attests to more than imaginary delusions

27. **constancy:** consistency, unchangingness

28. **howsoever:** i.e., in any case; **admirable:** i.e., worthy of wonder

32. **More:** i.e., more joy

33. **Wait . . . your board:** i.e., await you . . . your table

34. **masques:** like **revels** (line 39), a name for courtly entertainment

37. **after-supper:** a light meal or dessert served after the main supper

43. **abridgment:** i.e., pastime (to abridge or shorten the evening)

46. **brief:** i.e., list, short account; **sports:** diversions; **ripe:** ready, prepared

It comprehends some bringer of that joy.
Or in the night, imagining some fear,
How easy is a bush supposed a bear!
HIPPOLYTA
But all the story of the night told over,
And all their minds transfigured so together,   25
More witnesseth than fancy's images
And grows to something of great constancy,
But, howsoever, strange and admirable.

Enter Lovers: Lysander, Demetrius, Hermia, and Helena.

THESEUS
Here come the lovers full of joy and mirth.—
Joy, gentle friends! Joy and fresh days of love   30
Accompany your hearts!
LYSANDER   More than to us
Wait in your royal walks, your board, your bed!
THESEUS
Come now, what masques, what dances shall we
    have   35
To wear away this long age of three hours
Between ⌐our⌐ after-supper and bedtime?
Where is our usual manager of mirth?
What revels are in hand? Is there no play
To ease the anguish of a torturing hour?   40
Call Philostrate.
PHILOSTRATE, ⌐*coming forward*⌐
                    Here, mighty Theseus.
THESEUS
Say what abridgment have you for this evening,
What masque, what music? How shall we beguile
The lazy time if not with some delight?   45
PHILOSTRATE, ⌐*giving Theseus a paper*⌐
There is a brief how many sports are ripe.
Make choice of which your Highness will see first.

48. **battle with the Centaurs:** a famous incident in the life of Hercules

50. **We'll none:** i.e., we'll have none

51. **my kinsman:** Plutarch's "Life of Theseus" says that Hercules was Theseus's cousin.

52–53. **The riot . . . rage:** This would be the story of Orpheus (**the Thracian singer**) who was torn to pieces by women who worshiped Bacchus.

54. **device:** show, entertainment

56–57. **The thrice . . . beggary:** presumably a satirical play about the neglect of scholarship and learning. **thrice-three Muses:** The nine muses presided over literature, arts, and sciences. (See page 164.)

58. **critical:** judgmental

59. **sorting with:** i.e., suitable for, appropriate to

74. **passion of loud laughter:** i.e., intense or vehement laughter

78. **toiled:** fatigued, worn out; **unbreathed:** i.e., unexercised

79. **against:** i.e., in time for

THESEUS
   "The battle with the Centaurs, to be sung
   By an Athenian eunuch to the harp."
   We'll none of that. That have I told my love   50
   In glory of my kinsman Hercules.
   "The riot of the tipsy Bacchanals,
   Tearing the Thracian singer in their rage."
   That is an old device, and it was played
   When I from Thebes came last a conqueror.   55
   "The thrice-three Muses mourning for the death
   Of learning, late deceased in beggary."
   That is some satire, keen and critical,
   Not sorting with a nuptial ceremony.
   "A tedious brief scene of young Pyramus   60
   And his love Thisbe, very tragical mirth."
   "Merry" and "tragical"? "Tedious" and "brief"?
   That is hot ice and wondrous strange snow!
   How shall we find the concord of this discord?
PHILOSTRATE
   A play there is, my lord, some ten words long   65
   (Which is as brief as I have known a play),
   But by ten words, my lord, it is too long,
   Which makes it tedious; for in all the play,
   There is not one word apt, one player fitted.
   And tragical, my noble lord, it is.   70
   For Pyramus therein doth kill himself,
   Which, when I saw rehearsed, I must confess,
   Made mine eyes water; but more merry tears
   The passion of loud laughter never shed.
THESEUS
   What are they that do play it?   75
PHILOSTRATE
   Hard-handed men that work in Athens here,
   Which never labored in their minds till now,
   And now have toiled their unbreathed memories
   With this same play, against your nuptial.

85. **conned:** memorized

89. **simpleness:** sincerity; lack of sophistication

91. **wretchedness:** i.e., poor wretches; **o'er-charged:** overburdened

92. **his:** i.e., its

96. **take:** accept

97. **noble respect:** i.e., a generous regard or consideration

98. **Takes . . . merit:** i.e., perhaps, considers the effort, not the effect

99. **come:** i.e., journeyed; **clerks:** scholars

100. **premeditated:** previously designed

102. **periods:** i.e., stops

103. **their practiced accent:** i.e., the emphasis they had rehearsed

104. **dumbly:** silently

107. **fearful:** frightened

THESEUS
  And we will hear it.   80
PHILOSTRATE   No, my noble lord,
  It is not for you. I have heard it over,
  And it is nothing, nothing in the world,
  Unless you can find sport in their intents,
  Extremely stretched and conned with cruel pain   85
  To do you service.
THESEUS   I will hear that play,
  For never anything can be amiss
  When simpleness and duty tender it.
  Go, bring them in—and take your places, ladies.   90
                              ⌜*Philostrate exits.*⌝
HIPPOLYTA
  I love not to see wretchedness o'ercharged,
  And duty in his service perishing.
THESEUS
  Why, gentle sweet, you shall see no such thing.
HIPPOLYTA
  He says they can do nothing in this kind.
THESEUS
  The kinder we, to give them thanks for nothing.   95
  Our sport shall be to take what they mistake;
  And what poor duty cannot do, noble respect
  Takes it in might, not merit.
  Where I have come, great clerks have purposèd
  To greet me with premeditated welcomes,   100
  Where I have seen them shiver and look pale,
  Make periods in the midst of sentences,
  Throttle their practiced accent in their fears,
  And in conclusion dumbly have broke off,
  Not paying me a welcome. Trust me, sweet,   105
  Out of this silence yet I picked a welcome,
  And in the modesty of fearful duty,
  I read as much as from the rattling tongue
  Of saucy and audacious eloquence.

111. **to my capacity:** perhaps, in my opinion

112. **addressed:** ready

114–24. **If . . . know:** The comic effect of this prologue depends on its being delivered with the major pauses in the wrong places, in just the way that Theseus had earlier described.

117. **end:** aim, purpose

119. **minding:** i.e., intending

125. **stand upon points:** (1) is not a stickler for detail; (2) pays no attention to punctuation

126. **rid:** i.e., ridden; **rough:** i.e., untrained

127. **stop:** (1) signal to stop; (2) punctuation mark

130. **recorder:** a flutelike musical instrument

130–31. **in government:** i.e., controlled

132–33. **nothing:** not at all

Love, therefore, and tongue-tied simplicity   110
In least speak most, to my capacity.

⌐*Enter Philostrate.*⌐

PHILOSTRATE
So please your Grace, the Prologue is addressed.
THESEUS   Let him approach.

Enter the Prologue.

PROLOGUE
If we offend, it is with our goodwill.
    That you should think we come not to offend,   115
But with goodwill. To show our simple skill,
    That is the true beginning of our end.
Consider, then, we come but in despite.
    We do not come, as minding to content you,
Our true intent is. All for your delight   120
    We are not here. That you should here repent
        you,
The actors are at hand, and, by their show,
You shall know all that you are like to know.
                                   ⌐*Prologue exits.*⌐
THESEUS   This fellow doth not stand upon points.   125
LYSANDER   He hath rid his prologue like a rough colt;
    he knows not the stop. A good moral, my lord: it is
    not enough to speak, but to speak true.
HIPPOLYTA   Indeed he hath played on this prologue like
    a child on a recorder—a sound, but not in govern-   130
    ment.
THESEUS   His speech was like a tangled chain—noth-
    ing impaired, but all disordered. Who is next?

Enter Pyramus ⌐*(Bottom),*⌐ *and Thisbe* ⌐*(Flute),*⌐ *and*
Wall ⌐*(Snout),*⌐ *and Moonshine* ⌐*(Starveling),*⌐ *and Lion*
                ⌐*(Snug),*⌐ ⌐*and Prologue (Quince).*⌐

QUINCE, *as Prologue*
Gentles, perchance you wonder at this show.

148. **hight:** is called
151. **fall:** i.e., drop
153. **tall:** brave
156. **broached:** i.e., stabbed (with a comic allusion
to "broaching [i.e., tapping] a keg of beer or wine")
160. **At large:** i.e., at length

Pyramus and Thisbe. (5.1.136–37)
From Ovid, *Le metamorphosi* . . . (1538).

But wonder on, till truth make all things plain.   135
This man is Pyramus, if you would know.
  This beauteous lady Thisbe is certain.
This man with lime and roughcast doth present
  "Wall," that vile wall which did these lovers
    sunder;   140
And through Wall's chink, poor souls, they are
    content
  To whisper, at the which let no man wonder.
This man, with lantern, dog, and bush of thorn,
  Presenteth "Moonshine," for, if you will know,   145
By moonshine did these lovers think no scorn
  To meet at Ninus' tomb, there, there to woo.
This grisly beast (which "Lion" hight by name)
  The trusty Thisbe coming first by night
Did ⌜scare⌝ away, or rather did affright;   150
And, as she fled, her mantle she did fall,
  Which Lion vile with bloody mouth did stain.
Anon comes Pyramus, sweet youth and tall,
  And finds his trusty Thisbe's mantle slain.
Whereat, with blade, with bloody blameful blade,   155
  He bravely broached his boiling bloody breast.
And Thisbe, tarrying in mulberry shade,
  His dagger drew, and died. For all the rest,
Let Lion, Moonshine, Wall, and lovers twain
At large discourse, while here they do remain.   160
THESEUS   I wonder if the lion be to speak.
DEMETRIUS   No wonder, my lord. One lion may when
    many asses do.
          Lion, Thisbe, Moonshine, ⌜and Prologue⌝ exit.
SNOUT, *as Wall*
  In this same interlude it doth befall
  That I, one ⌜Snout⌝ by name, present a wall;   165
  And such a wall as I would have you think
  That had in it a crannied hole or chink,
  Through which the lovers, Pyramus and Thisbe,

172. **sinister:** left (Here, in performance, "Wall" usually makes a "cranny" by holding his fingers in the shape of a V.)

174. **lime and hair:** the materials that make up roughcast

176. **wittiest:** most intelligent

188. **eyne:** i.e., eyes

189. **Thanks:** in response to Wall's gesture of showing the cranny; **Jove shield thee:** i.e., God reward you

194. **being sensible:** i.e., having senses

195. **curse again:** i.e., return the curse

198–99. **fall pat:** i.e., happen exactly

Did whisper often, very secretly.
This loam, this roughcast, and this stone doth show   170
That I am that same wall. The truth is so.
And this the cranny is, right and sinister,
Through which the fearful lovers are to whisper.
THESEUS   Would you desire lime and hair to speak
  better?   175
DEMETRIUS   It is the wittiest partition that ever I heard
  discourse, my lord.
THESEUS   Pyramus draws near the wall. Silence.
BOTTOM, *as Pyramus*
  O grim-looked night! O night with hue so black!
    O night, which ever art when day is not!   180
  O night! O night! Alack, alack, alack!
    I fear my Thisbe's promise is forgot.
  And thou, O wall, O sweet, O lovely wall,
    That stand'st between her father's ground and
      mine,   185
  Thou wall, O wall, O sweet and lovely wall,
    Show me thy chink to blink through with mine
      eyne.
  Thanks, courteous wall. Jove shield thee well for
    this.   190
    But what see I? No Thisbe do I see.
  O wicked wall, through whom I see no bliss,
    Cursed be thy stones for thus deceiving me!
THESEUS   The wall, methinks, being sensible, should
  curse again.   195
BOTTOM   No, in truth, sir, he should not. "Deceiving
  me" is Thisbe's cue. She is to enter now, and I am
  to spy her through the wall. You shall see it will fall
  pat as I told you. Yonder she comes.

                Enter Thisbe ⌜*(Flute).*⌝

FLUTE, *as Thisbe*
  O wall, full often hast thou heard my moans   200

205. **an:** if

209. **Limander:** no doubt "Leander," a famous lover

210. **Helen:** perhaps, Helen of Troy (One would think that the name here should have been Hero, Leander's love.)

211. **Shafalus, Procrus:** no doubt Cephalus and Procris, famous tragic lovers

215. **Ninny's tomb:** i.e., Ninus's tomb (See page 74, note to line 97.)

216. **'Tide . . . death:** i.e., come life or death **'Tide:** betide

217. **dischargèd:** performed

222. **to:** i.e., as to

224. **in this kind:** i.e., plays and/or players; **shadows:** illusions, fictions

For parting my fair Pyramus and me.
My cherry lips have often kissed thy stones,
  Thy stones with lime and hair knit ⌜up in thee.⌝
BOTTOM, *as Pyramus*
I see a voice! Now will I to the chink
  To spy an I can hear my Thisbe's face.   205
Thisbe?
FLUTE, *as Thisbe*
        My love! Thou art my love, I think.
BOTTOM, *as Pyramus*
  Think what thou wilt, I am thy lover's grace,
And, like Limander, am I trusty still.
FLUTE, *as Thisbe*
And I like Helen, till the Fates me kill.   210
BOTTOM, *as Pyramus*
Not Shafalus to Procrus was so true.
FLUTE, *as Thisbe*
As Shafalus to Procrus, I to you.
BOTTOM, *as Pyramus*
O kiss me through the hole of this vile wall.
FLUTE, *as Thisbe*
I kiss the wall's hole, not your lips at all.
BOTTOM, *as Pyramus*
Wilt thou at Ninny's tomb meet me straightway?   215
FLUTE, *as Thisbe*
'Tide life, 'tide death, I come without delay.
                        ⌜*Bottom and Flute exit.*⌝
SNOUT, *as Wall*
  Thus have I, Wall, my part dischargèd so,
  And, being done, thus Wall away doth go. ⌜*He exits.*⌝
THESEUS Now is the ⌜wall down⌝ between the two
  neighbors.   220
DEMETRIUS No remedy, my lord, when walls are so
  willful to hear without warning.
HIPPOLYTA This is the silliest stuff that ever I heard.
THESEUS The best in this kind are but shadows, and

238. **A lion . . . dam:** perhaps, am neither a lion nor a lioness   **fell:** fierce   **dam:** mother

254–55. **horns . . . head:** a reference to the cuckold

256. **no crescent:** i.e., not a crescent (waxing, growing) moon

A "horned man," or cuckold. (5.1.254–55)
From *Bagford Ballads* (printed in 1878).

the worst are no worse, if imagination amend   225
them.
HIPPOLYTA   It must be your imagination, then, and not
theirs.
THESEUS   If we imagine no worse of them than they of
themselves, they may pass for excellent men. Here   230
come two noble beasts in, a man and a lion.

Enter Lion ⌜*(Snug)*⌝ *and Moonshine* ⌜*(Starveling).*⌝

SNUG, *as Lion*
You ladies, you whose gentle hearts do fear
The smallest monstrous mouse that creeps on
floor,
May now perchance both quake and tremble here,   235
When lion rough in wildest rage doth roar.
Then know that I, as Snug the joiner, am
A lion fell, nor else no lion's dam;
For if I should as lion come in strife
Into this place, 'twere pity on my life.   240
THESEUS   A very gentle beast, and of a good con-
science.
DEMETRIUS   The very best at a beast, my lord, that e'er I
saw.
LYSANDER   This lion is a very fox for his valor.   245
THESEUS   True, and a goose for his discretion.
DEMETRIUS   Not so, my lord, for his valor cannot carry
his discretion, and the fox carries the goose.
THESEUS   His discretion, I am sure, cannot carry his
valor, for the goose carries not the fox. It is well.   250
Leave it to his discretion, and let us listen to the
Moon.
STARVELING, *as Moonshine*
This lanthorn doth the hornèd moon present.
DEMETRIUS   He should have worn the horns on his
head.   255
THESEUS   He is no crescent, and his horns are invisible
within the circumference.

263. **for the candle:** i.e., for fear of the candle

264. **in snuff:** i.e., (1) in need of having its wick trimmed; (2) angry

269. **stay:** wait for

284. **moused:** torn or shaken (as a cat with a mouse)

STARVELING, *as Moonshine*
  This lanthorn doth the hornèd moon present.
  Myself the man i' th' moon do seem to be.
THESEUS This is the greatest error of all the rest; the 260
  man should be put into the lanthorn. How is it else
  "the man i' th' moon"?
DEMETRIUS He dares not come there for the candle,
  for you see, it is already in snuff.
HIPPOLYTA I am aweary of this moon. Would he would 265
  change.
THESEUS It appears by his small light of discretion that
  he is in the wane; but yet, in courtesy, in all reason,
  we must stay the time.
LYSANDER Proceed, Moon. 270
STARVELING, *as Moonshine* All that I have to say is to tell
  you that the lanthorn is the moon, I the man i' th'
  moon, this thornbush my thornbush, and this dog
  my dog.
DEMETRIUS Why, all these should be in the lanthorn, 275
  for all these are in the moon. But silence. Here
  comes Thisbe.

Enter Thisbe ⌐(Flute).⌐

FLUTE, *as Thisbe*
  This is old Ninny's tomb. Where is my love?
SNUG, *as Lion* O!
               ⌐*The Lion roars. Thisbe runs off,*
                        dropping her mantle.⌐
DEMETRIUS Well roared, Lion. 280
THESEUS Well run, Thisbe.
HIPPOLYTA Well shone, Moon. Truly, the Moon shines
  with a good grace.
                   ⌐*Lion worries the mantle.*⌐
THESEUS Well moused, Lion.

Enter Pyramus ⌐(Bottom).⌐

293. **dole:** sorrow

299. **Furies:** the Erinys, mythological beings who punished those who offended against natural and moral laws; **fell:** fierce

300. **Fates:** In Greek mythology, the three Fates wove one's life and brought about one's death by cutting life's thread.

301. **thread and thrum:** i.e., the whole thread of my life   **thrum:** the tufted end of the warp

302. **Quail:** overcome; **quell:** kill

303. **passion:** i.e., staging of strong emotion

305. **Beshrew:** i.e., curse

306. **wherefore:** why

307. **deflowered:** a malapropism, or verbal confusion, perhaps for "devoured"

309–10. **with cheer:** i.e., with her face; also, perhaps, cheerfully

311. **confound:** destroy

313. **pap:** breast (usually used to refer to the nipple or breast of a woman or the teat of an animal)

DEMETRIUS   And then came Pyramus.   285
⌜*Lion exits.*⌝

LYSANDER   And so the lion vanished.
BOTTOM, *as Pyramus*
Sweet Moon, I thank thee for thy sunny beams.
I thank thee, Moon, for shining now so bright,
For by thy gracious, golden, glittering ⌜gleams,⌝
I trust to take of truest Thisbe sight.—   290
But stay! O spite!
But mark, poor knight,
What dreadful dole is here!
Eyes, do you see!
How can it be!   295
O dainty duck! O dear!
Thy mantle good—
What, stained with blood?
Approach, ye Furies fell!
O Fates, come, come,   300
Cut thread and thrum,
Quail, crush, conclude, and quell!
THESEUS   This passion, and the death of a dear friend,
would go near to make a man look sad.
HIPPOLYTA   Beshrew my heart but I pity the man.   305
BOTTOM, *as Pyramus*
O, wherefore, Nature, didst thou lions frame,
Since lion vile hath here deflowered my dear,
Which is—no, no—which was the fairest dame
That lived, that loved, that liked, that looked with
cheer?   310
Come, tears, confound!
Out, sword, and wound
The pap of Pyramus;
Ay, that left pap,
Where heart doth hop. ⌜*Pyramus stabs himself.*⌝ 315
Thus die I, thus, thus, thus.
Now am I dead;

323. **die:** one of a pair of dice   **ace:** a one-spot on a die

328. **ass:** perhaps a pun on the earlier **ace**

329. **How chance Moonshine is:** i.e., why has Moonshine

340. **means:** (1) moans, laments; (2) lodges a formal complaint; **videlicet:** to wit, as follows

344. **dumb:** silent

"The thrice-three Muses." (5.1.56)
From Natale Conti, *Natalis Comitis Mythologiae* . . . (1616).

    Now am I fled;
My soul is in the sky.
    Tongue, lose thy light!   320
    Moon, take thy flight!   ⌜*Moonshine exits.*⌝
Now die, die, die, die, die.   ⌜*Pyramus falls.*⌝
DEMETRIUS No die, but an ace, for him, for he is but
    one.
LYSANDER Less than an ace, man, for he is dead, he is 325
    nothing.
THESEUS With the help of a surgeon he might yet
    recover and yet prove an ass.
HIPPOLYTA How chance Moonshine is gone before
    Thisbe comes back and finds her lover?   330
THESEUS She will find him by starlight.

                ⌜*Enter Thisbe (Flute).*⌝

Here she comes, and her passion ends the play.
HIPPOLYTA Methinks she should not use a long one for
    such a Pyramus. I hope she will be brief.
DEMETRIUS A mote will turn the balance, which Pyra- 335
    mus, which Thisbe, is the better: he for a man, God
    warrant us; she for a woman, God bless us.
LYSANDER She hath spied him already with those
    sweet eyes.
DEMETRIUS And thus she means, *videlicet*—   340
FLUTE, *as Thisbe*
            Asleep, my love?
            What, dead, my dove?
        O Pyramus, arise!
            Speak, speak. Quite dumb?
            Dead? Dead? A tomb   345
        Must cover thy sweet eyes.
            These lily lips,
            This cherry nose,
        These yellow cowslip cheeks
            Are gone, are gone!   350

353. **Sisters Three:** i.e., the Fates

357. **shore:** i.e., shorn, cut (phrased to rhyme with **gore**)

358. **thread of silk:** i.e., the thread of his life (phrased to rhyme with **milk**)

361. **imbrue:** drench with blood

369–70. **see . . . hear:** Once again, Bottom confuses the senses of seeing and hearing.

370. **Bergomask dance:** a rustic dance

377–78. **discharged:** performed

380. **iron tongue of midnight:** i.e., the midnight bell (with its iron clapper)   **told:** counted out

381. **fairy time:** i.e., the time between midnight and dawn

382. **outsleep:** i.e., sleep past, oversleep

383. **overwatched:** i.e., stayed up so late

    Lovers, make moan;
His eyes were green as leeks.
    O Sisters Three,
    Come, come to me
With hands as pale as milk.   355
    Lay them in gore,
    Since you have shore
With shears his thread of silk.
    Tongue, not a word!
    Come, trusty sword,   360
Come, blade, my breast imbrue!
                 ⌜*Thisbe stabs herself.*⌝
And farewell, friends.
Thus Thisbe ends.
Adieu, adieu, adieu.   ⌜*Thisbe falls.*⌝

THESEUS Moonshine and Lion are left to bury the 365
  dead.

DEMETRIUS Ay, and Wall too.
                ⌜*Bottom and Flute arise.*⌝

⌜BOTTOM⌝ No, I assure you, the wall is down that
  parted their fathers. Will it please you to see the
  Epilogue or to hear a Bergomask dance between 370
  two of our company?

THESEUS No epilogue, I pray you. For your play needs
  no excuse. Never excuse. For when the players are
  all dead, there need none to be blamed. Marry, if
  he that writ it had played Pyramus and hanged 375
  himself in Thisbe's garter, it would have been a fine
  tragedy; and so it is, truly, and very notably discharged. But, come, your Bergomask. Let your
  epilogue alone.
            ⌜*Dance, and the players exit.*⌝

The iron tongue of midnight hath told twelve. 380
Lovers, to bed! 'Tis almost fairy time.
I fear we shall outsleep the coming morn
As much as we this night have overwatched.

384. **palpable-gross:** i.e., obviously dull
385. **heavy gait:** slow pace
386. **solemnity:** festive celebration
390. **heavy:** sleepy
391. **fordone:** exhausted
392. **wasted brands:** burned-up logs
394–95. **Puts . . . In remembrance of:** causes
. . . to think
398. **his:** i.e., its
401. **triple Hecate:** The goddess Hecate had three
forms (Luna, the moon, in the sky, Diana on earth,
and Proserpina in the underworld).
404. **frolic:** frolicsome, merry

This palpable-gross play hath well beguiled
The heavy gait of night. Sweet friends, to bed.   385
A fortnight hold we this solemnity
In nightly revels and new jollity.   *They exit.*

         Enter ⌐Robin Goodfellow.⌐

ROBIN
     Now the hungry ⌐lion⌐ roars,
          And the wolf ⌐behowls⌐ the moon,
     Whilst the heavy plowman snores,   390
          All with weary task fordone.
     Now the wasted brands do glow,
          Whilst the screech-owl, screeching loud,
     Puts the wretch that lies in woe
          In remembrance of a shroud.   395
     Now it is the time of night
          That the graves, all gaping wide,
     Every one lets forth his sprite
          In the church-way paths to glide.
     And we fairies, that do run   400
          By the triple Hecate's team
     From the presence of the sun,
          Following darkness like a dream,
     Now are frolic. Not a mouse
     Shall disturb this hallowed house.   405
     I am sent with broom before,
     To sweep the dust behind the door.

Enter ⌐Oberon and Titania,⌐ King and Queen of Fairies,
          with all their train.

OBERON
     Through the house give glimmering light,
          By the dead and drowsy fire.
     Every elf and fairy sprite,   410
          Hop as light as bird from brier,
     And this ditty after me,
     Sing and dance it trippingly.

420. **will we:** i.e., Titania and I will go
422. **there create:** i.e., created there
426. **the blots of Nature's hand:** i.e., deformities
427. **in their issue stand:** appear in their offspring
429. **prodigious:** ominous; abnormal
432. **field-dew consecrate:** i.e., consecrated dew
434. **several:** separate, individual
440. **shadows:** illusions; actors
444. **idle:** trivial

TITANIA

 First rehearse your song by rote,
 To each word a warbling note.   415
 Hand in hand, with fairy grace,
 Will we sing and bless this place.
  ⌜*Oberon leads the Fairies in song and dance.*⌝

OBERON

 Now, until the break of day,
 Through this house each fairy stray.
 To the best bride-bed will we,   420
 Which by us shall blessèd be,
 And the issue there create
 Ever shall be fortunate.
 So shall all the couples three
 Ever true in loving be,   425
 And the blots of Nature's hand
 Shall not in their issue stand.
 Never mole, harelip, nor scar,
 Nor mark prodigious, such as are
 Despisèd in nativity,   430
 Shall upon their children be.
 With this field-dew consecrate
 Every fairy take his gait,
 And each several chamber bless,
 Through this palace, with sweet peace. 435
 And the owner of it blest,
 Ever shall in safety rest.
 Trip away. Make no stay.
 Meet me all by break of day.
      ⌜*All but Robin*⌝ *exit.*

ROBIN

 If we shadows have offended,   440
 Think but this and all is mended:
 That you have but slumbered here
 While these visions did appear.
 And this weak and idle theme,

445. **No . . . dream:** i.e., producing no more than a dream

447. **mend:** improve

450. **serpent's tongue:** i.e., hisses (from the audience)

454. **Give me your hands:** i.e., applaud

No more yielding but a dream,   445
Gentles, do not reprehend.
If you pardon, we will mend.
And, as I am an honest Puck,
If we have unearnèd luck
Now to 'scape the serpent's tongue,   450
We will make amends ere long.
Else the Puck a liar call.
So good night unto you all.
Give me your hands, if we be friends,
And Robin shall restore amends.   455

⌜*He exits.*⌝

Textual Notes

The reading of the present text appears to the left of the square bracket. The earliest sources of readings not in **Q1,** the quarto of 1600, upon which this edition is based, are indicated as follows: **Q2** is the quarto of 1619; **Qq** is "Q1 and Q2"; **F** is the Shakespeare First Folio of 1623, in which *A Midsummer Night's Dream* is a slightly edited reprint of Q2. **Ed.** is an earlier editor of Shakespeare, from the editor of the Second Folio of 1632 to the present. No sources are given for emendations of punctuation or for correction of obvious typographical errors, such as turned letters that produce no known word. **SD** means stage direction; **SP** means speech heading; ~ refers to a word already quoted.

1.1	4. wanes] Q2, F; waues Q1
	10. New] Ed.; Now Qq, F
	20. SD *Lysander and*] F; Lysander *and* Helena, *and* Qq
	25, 27. Stand forth, Demetrius . . . Stand forth, Lysander] Ed.; *set as stage directions in* Qq, F
	138. low] Ed.; loue Qq, F
	154. patience] patienee Q1
	190. Yours would] Ed.; Your words Qq, F
	195. I'd] Ed.; ile Qq, F
	221. sweet] Ed.; sweld Qq, F
	224. stranger companies] Ed.; strange companions Qq, F
	229. SD *1 line earlier in* Qq, F
1.2	1. SP QUINCE] *Qnin.* Q1
	26. rest.—Yet] ~ ⌃ ~, Qq, F
	28–29. split: / *The*] Ed.; split the Qq, F

43. SP FLUTE] *Fla.* Q1

2.1   63 *and hereafter throughout Act 2.* SP TI-
TANIA] Ed.; *Qu.* Qq, F

63. Fairies] Ed.; Fairy Qq, F

71. steep] Q1 (steppe)

81. Perigouna] Ed.; *Perigenia* Qq, F

82. Aegles] Ed.; Eagles Qq, F

112. thin] Ed.; chinne Qq, F

158. certain] cettain Q1

160 *and hereafter in Act 2.* SP ROBIN] Ed.;
Puck. Qq, F

164. the] F; *omit* Q

190. off] Q (of)

201. thee] Q (the)

208. not, nor] F; not, not Qq

253. SD *Robin*] Ed.; Pucke Qq, F; SD *1 line
later in* Qq, F

2.2   9. SP FIRST FAIRY] Ed.; *omit* Qq, F

13, 24. SP CHORUS] Ed.; *omit* Qq, F

24–30. *Philomel . . . lullaby*] Ed.; *Philomele* with
melody, &c. Qq, F

44. comfort] comfor Q1

45. Be] Q2, F; Bet Q1

49. good] Q1 (god)

53. is] Q2, F; it Q1

71. SD *Robin*] Ed.; Pucke Qq, F

156. Methought] Me thoughr Q1

3.1   8. SP QUINCE] *Qnin.* Q1

50. SP SNOUT] Q1 (*Sn.*)

55. SP BOTTOM] Q2, F; *Cet.* Q1

73. your] yonr Q1

81, 83, 104. SP BOTTOM, *as Pyramus*] Ed.; *Pyra.* Qq, F

82. odors] F; odorous Qq

87. SP ROBIN.] F (*Puck*); *Quin.* Qq

88. SP FLUTE] Ed.; *Thys.* Qq, F

92. SP FLUTE, *as Thisbe*] Ed.; *Thys.* Qq, F

101. SP FLUTE] Ed.; *Thys.* Qq, F
103. SD *after line 113 in* F *"Enter Piramus with the Asse head"; omit* Q1
104. fair Thisbe] Ed.; *Thysby* Qq, F
106. SD *Quince . . . exit.] omit* Qq; *The Clownes all Exit.* F
164. SD *Enter foure Fairyes.* Qq; *Enter Peaseblossome, Cobweb, Moth, Mustardseede, and foure Fairies.* F
165. SP PEASEBLOSSOM] Ed.; *Fairies.* Qq, F
166. SP COBWEB] Ed.; *omit* Qq, F
167. SP MOTE] Ed.; *omit* Qq, F
168. SP MUSTARDSEED] Ed.; *omit* Qq, F
169. SP ALL] Ed.; *omit* Qq, F
181. SP PEASEBLOSSOM] Ed.; *1. Fai.* Qq, F
182. SP COBWEB] Ed.; *omit* Qq, F
183. SP MOTE] Ed.; *2. Fai.* Qq, F
184. SP MUSTARDSEED] Ed.; *3.Fai.* Qq, F
202. of] Ed.; *omit* Qq, F

3.2   0. SD *Enter . . . Fairies.*] F (*adding* "solus"); Qq (*adding* "and Robin goodfellow.")
3. SD *Enter . . . Goodfellow.*] F (*Enter Pucke.*); *omit* Qq
6. SP ROBIN] Ed.; *Puck* Qq, F
6–7. love. . . . bower,] ~, . . . ~. Q1; ~, . . . ~, Q2, F
19. mimic] F; Minnick Q1; Minnock Q2
54. From] Frow Q1
82. so] Ed.; *omit* Qq, F
86. grow‸] ~. Q1
87. sleep] Ed.; slippe Qq, F
111. SD *Robin*] Puck Qq, F
112 *and hereafter until line 418.* SP ROBIN] *Puck* Qq, F
140. *waking up*] F (*Awa.*) *after* l. 139; *omit* Qq

162. derision! None] Ed.; ~ ˄ ~ Q1; ~,~ Q2,
     ~;~ F
218. first, like] Ed.; first life Qq, F
244. sweet] sweeete Q1
257. prayers] Ed.; praise Qq, F
270. off] Q1 (of)
293. Therefore] Thefore Q1
314. gentlemen] Q2, F; gentleman Q1
343. but] Q2, F; hut Q1
365. SD *She exits.] Exeunt.* Qq; *omit* F
369. should] shoud Q1
416. notwithstanding] notwiststanding Q1
430. Speak!] Ed.; ~ ˄ Qq, F
454. shalt] shat Q1
470. SD *1 line earlier in* F
480. To] Ed.; *omit* Qq, F

4.1   0. SD *Bottom]* Ed.; *Clowne* Qq, F. *At the
         end of Act 3* F *reads* "They sleepe all the
         Act."
         5 *and throughout scene.* SP BOTTOM] Ed.;
         Clown. Qq, F
        30. F *prints* SD "Musicke Tongs, Rurall Mu-
            sicke."
        42. all ways] Q1 (alwaies)
        74. o'er] Q1 (or)
        84. sleep˄ . . . these five] Ed.; sleepe: . . .
            these, fine Qq, F
        85. F *prints* SD "Musick still."
       105. F *prints* SD "Sleepers Lye still."
       106. SD *Oberon . . . Egeus.] Exeunt. Enter
            Theseus and all his traine. Winde
            horne.* Qq; *Exeunt. Winde Hornes. En-
            ter Theseus, Egeus, Hippolita and all
            his traine.* F
       121. Seemed] Ed.; Seeme Qq, F
       133. is] Q2, F; *omit* Q1
       138. rite] Q1 (right)

143. SD *Shout . . . up.*] *Shoute within: they all start vp. Winde hornes.* Qq; *Hornes and they wake. Shout within, they all start vp.* F
179. saw] Ed.; see Qq, F
193. SD *Theseus . . . exit.*] *Exit Duke and Lords.* F
199. found] Q1 (fonnd)
209. let us] Q2, F; lets Q1
210. SD *waking up*] F (*"Bottome wakes." after line 209*)
217. to] Q2, F; *omit* Q1
219. a patched] F; patcht a Qq

4.2 0. SD *Enter . . . Starveling.*] *Enter* Quince, Flute, Thisby *and the rabble.* Qq; *Enter Quince, Flute, Thisbie, Snout, and Starueling.* F
3. SP STARVELING] F; *Flut.* Qq
5 *and throughout scene.* SP FLUTE] Ed.; *Thys*[be] Qq, F

5.1 0. SD *Enter . . . Attendants.*] Q1; *Enter Theseus, Hippolita, Egeus and his Lords.* F
37. our] F; Or Qq
113. SP THESEUS] Ed.; *Duk.* Qq, F
113. SD F *begins with "Flor. Trum."*
133. SD F *begins with "Tawyer with a Trumpet before them."*
133. SD *Prologue (Quince)*] F *at 113 SD has "Prologue. Quince."*
134. SP QUINCE, *as Prologue*] Ed.; *Prologue* Qq, F
137. Thisbe] *Thsby* Q1
150. scare] Ed.; scarre Qq, F
163. SD *Lion . . . exit.*] Qq; *Exit all but Wall.* F, *3 lines earlier*
164 *and hereafter.* SP SNOUT, *as Wall*] Ed.; *Wall.* Qq, F

165. Snout] F; *Flute* Qq
178. F *prints "Enter Pyramus."*
179 *and hereafter.* SP BOTTOM, *as Pyramus*]
      Py. Qq, F
196. SP BOTTOM] Ed.; *Pyr.* Qq, F
200 *and hereafter.* SP FLUTE, *as Thisbe*] Ed.;
      This. Qq, F
203. hair] hayire Q1
203. up in thee] F; now againe Qq
218. SD *He exits.*] *Exit Clow.* F
219 *and hereafter.* SP THESEUS] Ed.; *Duk.* Qq,
      F
219. wall down] Ed.; morall downe F; Moon
      vsed Qq
223 *and hereafter.* SP HIPPOLYTA] Ed.; *Dutch.*
      Qq, F
231. beasts͜ in,] ~, ~͜ Qq, F
232 *and hereafter.* SP SNUG, *as Lion*] Ed.; *Lyon.*
      Qq, F
253 *and hereafter.* SP STARVELING, *as Moon-*
      shine] Ed.; *Moone.* Qq, F
278, 345. tomb] Q1 (tumbe)
279. SD *The . . . off*] F; *omit* Q1
284. SD *2 lines later in Q1*
289. gleams] Ed.; beames Qq, F
329–30. before͜ Thisbe] ~? ~ Qq, F
331. SD *1 line earlier in F*
337. warrant] Q1 (warnd)
368. SP BOTTOM] F; *Lyon* Qq
387. SD *Robin Goodfellow*] Ed.; Pucke Qq, F
388. SP ROBIN] Ed.; *Puck* Qq, F
388. lion] Ed.; Lyons Qq, F
389. behowls] Ed.; beholds Qq, F
418. SP OBERON] Qq; *The Song.* F
436–37. *lines transposed in* Qq, F
439. SD *All . . . exit.*] Ed.; *Exeunt.* Qq; *omit* F

A Midsummer Night's Dream:
A Modern Perspective

Catherine Belsey

When Bottom wakes up, near the end of *A Midsummer Night's Dream*, after spending a night of love with the queen of the fairies, this formerly masterful and garrulous figure is suddenly very nearly inarticulate. What could he say that would do justice to the experience? "I have had a most rare vision. I have had a dream past the wit of man to say what dream it was. Man is but an ass if he go about to expound this dream" (4.1.214–17). Bottom's name, and his transformation—an event that clarifies more than it changes his identity—invite the audience to associate him with the least poetic aspects of life, and yet, even as an ass, Bottom has been touched by something special but mysterious, a power that he finds unusually hard to define. In quest of a way of talking about what has happened to him, Bottom reaches for the language of the Bible, St. Paul's account of the future glory that God has prepared for human beings (1 Corinthians 2.9), though of course, being Bottom, he gets it wrong: "The eye of man hath not heard, the ear of man hath not seen, man's hand is not able to taste, his tongue to conceive, nor his heart to report what my dream was" (4.1.220–24). In the end he concludes that the solution is for Peter Quince to write a ballad of his dream. Evidently only the lyricism of popular poetry seems to Bottom adequate to define the experience of love.

We do not have Peter Quince's ballad, but—if we assume that Quince wrote "Pyramus and Thisbe," in which Bottom plays the romantic hero—we do have his play, and we also have Shakespeare's play, which is its

181

setting. *A Midsummer Night's Dream* is a play about love. It proposes that love is a dream, or perhaps a vision; that it is absurd, irrational, a delusion, or, perhaps, on the other hand, a transfiguration; that it is doomed to be momentary ("So quick bright things come to confusion" [1.1.151]), and that it constitutes at the same time the proper foundation for lifelong marriage. Possibly Bottom is right, the play suggests, not to pin down anything so multiple, not to encapsulate love in a neat definition that would encourage us to measure our own and other people's experience and find it normal or abnormal, mature or immature, wise or foolish. The play's device, on the contrary, is to dramatize the plurality of love by characterizing it differently in a range of distinct voices.

As soon as Hermia and Lysander are left alone together on the stage for the first time, they discuss their predicament in a series of elegant and elaborate exchanges:

LYSANDER
   How now, my love? Why is your cheek so pale?
   How chance the roses there do fade so fast?
HERMIA
   Belike for want of rain, which I could well
   Beteem them from the tempest of mine eyes.
                          (1.1.130–33)

Since the lovers and the audience have both heard Theseus tell Hermia that she must die or go into a convent if she refuses to marry another man, it is hardly necessary for Lysander to ask why she is pale, or for her to tell him that she thinks she might be going to cry. But the poetic image of the roses in her cheeks legitimates the conceit that follows: the roses are short of water, which Hermia is about to supply. The exchange has the effect of distancing the threat to Hermia, and putting before the audience instead what is delicate, lyrical, and witty in romance. Lysander's next utterance explains the way all four lovers tend to talk to each other:

> Ay me! For aught that I could ever read,
> Could ever hear by tale or history . . .
> (1.1.134–35)

How else, after all, do people learn to talk about love in the first instance, except by reading love stories? No wonder the four lovers are virtually indistinguishable. Romantic love is in this sense oddly impersonal. Because of love's power to idealize, the object of desire seems unique, even though in the event it turns out that Hermia and Helena are interchangeable. But the ways of idealizing, of investing the other person with the special beauty or magnetism that justifies desire, are drawn in the first place from the culture in which people learn about love.

Meanwhile Theseus, we are to understand, in contrast to the young lovers, has been around. The stories of his many loves and betrayals would have been well known, at least to those members of the audience who had been to school, and Oberon alludes to them in the course of his quarrel with Titania (2.1.81–83). Theseus himself talks quite differently about love:

> Now, fair Hippolyta, our nuptial hour
> Draws on apace. Four happy days bring in
> Another moon. But, O, methinks how slow
> This old moon wanes! She lingers my desires
> Like to a stepdame or a dowager
> Long withering out a young man's revenue.
> (1.1.1–6)

Theseus acknowledges that he has desires, and they are urgent and imperative. He is impatient with the moon, that conventional poetic symbol of romance, and the comparison he invokes is anything but lyrical. The moon that is delaying his marriage is like an old woman who refuses to die and so prevents her young heir from getting his hands on his inheritance. Paradoxically, the love that is voiced by Theseus seems more insistent to the degree that it is more prosaic, literally more like prose, since the speech rhythms do not coincide with the line endings, but run directly across them. The Amazon Hippolyta, whose comments so often counterpoint those of Theseus, immediately supplies the missing romance by reinvesting with its customary lyricism "the moon, like to a silver bow / New-bent in heaven" (1.1.9–10).[1]

The young lovers perfectly reproduce the conventional idealizing imagery of the period:

> O Helen, goddess, nymph, perfect, divine!
> To what, my love, shall I compare thine eyne?
> Crystal is muddy. O, how ripe in show
> Thy lips, those kissing cherries, tempting grow!
> That pure congealèd white, high Taurus' snow,
> Fanned with the eastern wind, turns to a crow
> When thou hold'st up thy hand.
>
> (3.2.140–46)

Eyes like crystals, lips like cherries, hands white as snow—this is engaging to the degree that it is lyrical. It is also delightfully absurd, when we bear in mind that it is the instant effect of Robin Goodfellow's love-juice, and represents a vision of Helena that Demetrius was quite unable to see before his sight was bewitched. But as Helena herself explains earlier in the play, love does not necessarily see what is there:

> Things base and vile, holding no quantity,
> Love can transpose to form and dignity.
> Love looks not with the eyes but with the mind;
> And therefore is winged Cupid painted blind.
> (1.1.238–41)

Helena's words might equally constitute a commentary on Titania's first response to Bottom braying in his ass's head: "What angel wakes me from my flow'ry bed?" (3.1.131). The fairy queen's temporary devotion to a donkey is the play's clearest and funniest indication of love's arbitrary nature.

One reason why the lovers seem comic is that their changes of preference do not appear arbitrary to them. As Lysander solemnly explains to his new love, Helena, "The will of man is by his reason swayed, / And reason says you are the worthier maid" (2.2.122–23). The element of absurdity is compounded when we recognize (though they do not) a parody of their idealizing vision in Thisbe's lament for the dead Pyramus:

> These lily lips,
> This cherry nose,
> These yellow cowslip cheeks
> Are gone, are gone!
> Lovers, make moan;
> His eyes were green as leeks.
> (5.1.347–52)

The king and queen of the fairies are old (or, rather, ageless) married lovers, and they are quarreling. The play does not ignore the trace of violence that exists within love when the other person fails to conform to the lover's idealized image. The quarrel between Oberon and Titania has upset the proper sequence of the seasons, which is a serious problem in a society based on agriculture, though it is hard for the audience to feel great anxiety about this when the fairies quarrel so musically:

> These are the forgeries of jealousy;
> And never, since the middle summer's spring,
> Met we on hill, in dale, forest, or mead,
> By pavèd fountain or by rushy brook,
> Or in the beachèd margent of the sea,
> To dance our ringlets to the whistling wind,
> But with thy brawls thou hast disturbed our sport.
>   (2.1.84–90)

The brawls are not mentioned until the verse has quite distracted us from the substance of the quarrel through its evocation of imaginary landscapes, so lacking in specific detail that they seem the settings of half-remembered legends and tales of adventure. No wonder Oberon and Titania are finally reconciled. In a similar way, lyricism and comedy distance the passionate quarrels between Demetrius and Lysander, Hermia and Helena. Conversely, if the play of "Pyramus and Thisbe" evokes tears of laughter rather than sorrow (5.1.73–74), it alludes, nevertheless, to the tragic possibilities of a conflict between love and parental opposition. *A Midsummer Night's Dream* does not let its audience forget that love entails confusion and danger as well as grace, although it never entirely separates these contraries.

None of the distinct voices in the play—romantic, lyrical, or urgent—seems to exhaust the character of love; none of them can be identified with "true" love as opposed to false. Nor does any of them summarize the nature of love; and when Theseus tries to do so, what he says seems quite inadequate. "I never may believe," he insists, "These antique fables, nor these fairy toys" (5.1.2–3). "Antique" implies both "ancient" and "antic" (theatrical), and ironically Theseus himself is both. He is a fictional hero of classical legend and a figure on a stage in the most theatrical of plays. As for the fairy stories he repudiates, we have seen them enacted in the course of the play, and we are therefore in no position to share his entirely rational dismissal of lovers, along with lunatics and poets (5.1.7). Hippolyta seems more to the point when she answers him, but she is considerably less than specific. The separate stories of the night, she affirms, grow "to something of great constancy [consistency], / But, howsoever, strange and admirable [eliciting wonder]" (5.1.27–28). In talking about love, as perhaps in love itself, there is commonly a sense of a quality that cannot be made present, cannot be presented, or represented. In the most exhaustive analysis, the most effusive declaration, or the most lyrical poem, something slips away, and it is that elusiveness that sustains desire itself, as well as the desire to talk about it.

And this, perhaps, is a clue to the nature of the pleasure *A Midsummer Night's Dream* offers its audience. It constructs for the spectators something of the desire it also puts on display. In one sense comedy produces the wishes it then goes on to fulfill. The play invites us to sympathize with the young lovers. In consequence, we want Hermia to marry the man she loves, in spite of the opposition of her ridiculous father, who supposes that serenades and love tokens are forms of witchcraft. And we want Helena to be happy with Demetrius in spite of his initial rejection of her love. The enigma that enlists the desire of the audience centers on whether the play will bring about the happy ending we hope for, and if so, how. The pleasure of this dramatic form is familiar from Roman comedy to Neil Simon, and its familiarity is precisely part of the enjoyment we are invited to experience.

But *A Midsummer Night's Dream* does not always do

exactly what we might expect, and in this way it keeps its audience guessing, continually reoffering itself in the process as an object of our desire. The play begins with the longing of Theseus and Hippolyta to consummate their love, and the action that follows occupies the intervening space, so that at the end of Act 5 the newly married lovers go off to bed together. Desire constitutes the frame of the play itself. In the meantime, Theseus dispatches the master of the revels, who is responsible for entertainment at court, in search of "merriments" and "reveling" (1.1.13, 20), and at once an old man comes in with his daughter and her two rival suitors. Egeus is appropriately stagy ("Stand forth, Demetrius . . . Stand forth, Lysander" [1.1.25, 27]), and the audience might be expected to recognize the pattern of Roman comedy, familiar from the plays of Plautus and Terence and widely imitated in Elizabethan drama. The conventional poetry and the extravagance of the lovers intensifies the sense that we are watching the first of the revels that Theseus has sent for, a play within a play.

But Roman comedy does not characteristically include fairies, and it is the mischief-making Robin Goodfellow, a supernatural figure from English folklore, who largely motivates the plot of this inset play. The genres are mixed, with the effect that the audience is never quite sure whether the conventions in operation at any specific moment are those of comedy or folktale. At the same time, Robin Goodfellow (Puck) both is and is not a native English replica of the blind, irrational, overhasty, and Continental Cupid that Helena describes. The play teases the audience with glimpses of familiar forms and figures, and then deflects our attention onto something unexpected. In consequence, the delight it invites the spectators to experience is entirely distinct from the comfortable feeling of recognition other plays rely on.

The plot leads up to the marriages of the lovers, but it does not quite confirm the distinction we might expect it to identify between true love on the one hand and arbitrary passion induced by magic on the other. Demetrius still has the love-juice on his eyes, and yet the play gives no indication of a difference between this marriage and the others. If marriage is a serious social institution, it seems to rest on a remarkably precarious base. But the imperatives of fiction require that the comedy of love end in marriage, and Demetrius marries the partner he has when the action comes to a stop.

If the story leads up to marriage, however, it does not quite end there. Many critical accounts of the play depend on an opposition between its two locations, the house of Theseus in Athens and the wildwood under the control of the fairies. The Athenian court represents the world of reconciliation and rationality, of social institutions and communal order, while the wood outside Athens is the location of night and bewildering passions, a place of anarchy and anxiety, where behavior becomes unpredictable and individual identity is transformed. On this reading, the fairies, who are by no means the sugary creatures of Victorian fantasy, represent the quintessence of all that is turbulent and uncontrolled in human experience, and in particular the traces of instability and violence that inhabit desire.

At the end of the play, however, when the couples, now properly distributed and legitimately married, have gone to bed, the fairies come in from the wood and take possession of the palace: "Through the house give glimmering light, / By the dead and drowsy fire . . ." (5.1.408–9). Though their purpose, we are to understand, is benevolent, they also bring with them the uncanny resonances of the dreamworld that seemed to have been left behind in the wood:

> . . . we fairies, that do run
>   By the triple Hecate's team
> From the presence of the sun,
>   Following darkness like a dream
> Now are frolic.
>
> (5.1.400–4)

Hecate is the queen of the night, and the team the fairies run with are the dragons who draw her chariot. Their unexpected presence within the house, therefore, implies the invasion of elements of the turbulent, the magical, and the unearthly into the social and domestic proprieties of marriage.

How could it be otherwise? This is, after all, a wedding night. But by handing over the conclusion to the fairies, the play displaces the apparent closure, the celebration of restored identity and the return to community it has duly delivered. Instead, it goes on to re-create what is most mysterious and elusive in the world it has portrayed, and gives the stage back to the representatives of all that is unaccountable and still unrecounted in the experience of love. In this way *A Midsummer Night's Dream* offers to leave its audience in a state of mind that bears some resemblance to Bottom's when he wakes up from *his* dream: exalted, perhaps, but a little less assured, less confident, and altogether less knowing than before.

---

1. It is possible, of course, that the new-bent bow is not merely lyrical. As an Amazon, Hippolyta would have carried a bow as a weapon against Theseus and his army. See James Calderwood's *"A Midsummer Night's Dream:* Anamorphism and Theseus' Dream," *Shakespeare Quarterly* 42 (1991): 409–30, esp. p. 413, for a discussion of Elizabethan attitudes toward Amazons.

Further Reading

A Midsummer Night's Dream

Barber, C. L. "May Games and Metamorphoses on a Midsummer Night." In *Shakespeare's Festive Comedy*, pp. 119–62. Princeton: Princeton University Press, 1959.

Barber proposes that Shakespeare's *Dream* involves a "complex fusion of pageantry and popular games." Mixed with the kind of pageantry usually presented at aristocratic weddings are the more popular rituals of May Day—a combination Shakespeare exploits to fashion the town-grove-town movement the play follows. By structuring the play around oppositions—everyday/holiday, town/grove, day/night—Shakespeare confidently separates "shadow" from "substance" and provides an environment of "unshadowed gaiety."

Barkan, Leonard. "Ovid Translated." In *The Gods Made Flesh: Metamorphosis and the Pursuit of Paganism*, pp. 251–70. New Haven: Yale University Press, 1986.

Focusing on Theseus's fifth-act dismissal of the lovers' stories as "antique fables," Barkan explores *Dream's* self-conscious awareness of the classical myths that inspire much of *Dream's* action. Specifically, Barkan examines Shakespeare's "translation" of Ovid's *Metamorphoses* into his own "mythic language." Barkan concludes that Shakespeare views antiquity through the eyes of Ovid and therefore constructs an Athens where "gods, mortals and heroes live in democratic proximity, intermingling via the perils and delights of love."

Bristol, Michael. "Wedding Feast and Charivari." In *Carnival and Theater: Plebeian Culture and the Structure of Authority in Renaissance England,* pp. 162–78. New York and London: Methuen, 1985.

   In Elizabethan England, marriage was a largely public matter, with questions of preference and personal desire open to public scrutiny. Bristol therefore reads "Pyramus and Thisby" as an inadvertent social critique of the wedding of Theseus and Hippolyta, in that the farce's admonitory effects do not depend on the unwitting company's knowledge. The burlesque counterfestivity of the drama—which invokes a complex fusion of festive customs—reveals the insubstantiality of social identity by ridiculing the desires and behaviors of the drama's upper-class audience.

Calderwood, James L. *"A Midsummer Night's Dream:* Anamorphism and Theseus' Dream." *Shakespeare Quarterly* 42 (1991): 409–30.

   Calderwood explores the broader implications of doubling in *Dream,* i.e., assigning to a single actor the parts of both Titania and Hippolyta and assigning to another the parts of both Theseus and Oberon, a widespread practice in recent productions. With wonderfully comic results, Calderwood speculates that the scenes in the woods may be read as "Theseus' dream," in which the anxieties and desires that he feels on the occasion of his imminent wedding to the Amazon Hippolyta are played out with Theseus and Hippolyta as the Fairy King and Queen.

Girard, René. "Myth and Ritual in Shakespeare: *A Midsummer Night's Dream."* In *Textual Strategies: Perspectives in Post-Structuralist Criticism,* ed. Josué V. Harari, pp. 29–45. Ithaca, N.Y.: Cornell University Press, 1979.

   Girard disentangles the relationship(s) among the four young lovers, finding the only constant to be the convergence of more than one desire on a single object, as if rivalry were more important than love. Girard determines that the driving desire is the absolute seductive dominance that each character in turn appears to embody in the eyes of the others. Their frantic attempt to "translate" themselves into the figure that, for the moment, possesses this sexual quality ultimately causes their differences to disintegrate and their identities to collapse.

Greer, Germaine. "Love and the Law." In *Politics, Power, and Shakespeare,* ed. Frances McNeely Leonard, pp. 29–45. Arlington, Texas: Texas Humanities Research Center, 1981.

Greer sets out the underlying conundrum of *Dream:* how to "civilize love," which is by nature "anarchic." Love and law meet, Greer writes, in marriage, and she therefore explores the unreliability of sexual passion as a basis for a lasting marriage as it is manifested in *Dream.* Rather than concluding with a "starry-eyed statement about living happily ever after," Shakespeare provides a pragmatic answer to *Dream*'s riddle in his appeal to "simple human dignity," in the persons of the mechanicals, and the responsibility of child rearing, as expressed in the play's marriage poem.

Leggatt, Alexander. *"A Midsummer Night's Dream."* In *Shakespeare's Comedy of Love,* pp. 89–115. London: Methuen, 1974.

Leggatt reads the play as a constant process of exorcism as each possible threat to the comic world is driven away. The slender separation between the comic world of the play and the darker world of "passion, terror and chaos" is maintained by the audience's empathy for the seemingly "trivial" concerns of the lovers. By taking the illusions of art and love as reality, the audience plays a vital part in *Dream*'s total harmony.

Marcus, Leah. *The Politics of Mirth: Jonson, Herrick, Milton, Marvell, and the Defense of Old Holiday Pastimes.* Chicago: University of Chicago Press, 1986.

Marcus traces the political struggle over the traditional pastimes of May Day and morris dances (both mentioned in *Dream*) that took place among Shakespeare's
contemporaries and successors. She places the festive
rituals associated with seasonal holidays within the
context of royal support for festive observances and
specific literary practice. The literature of festival, according to Marcus, attempted to meld art and life and
hence destroy its perceived separateness.

Miller, Ronald F. *"A Midsummer Night's Dream:* The
Fairies, Bottom, and the Mystery of Things." *Shakespeare Quarterly* 26 (1975): 254–68.
   Dream, for Miller, is a study of the nature and validity
of the imagination. The indefiniteness of the fairies
themselves calls into question the nature of love in
Dream, for if the fairies, who in Theseus's analysis are
the bringers of joy, are delusions, love is a delusion.
Ultimately, however, Bottom's speech upon waking
from his transformation—which echoes St. Paul's para-
dox that faith is both folly and the highest wisdom—
establishes the fairies' ambiguous existence within the
framework of a play that simultaneously encourages
credulity and skepticism.

Mowat, Barbara. "'A local habitation and a name':
Shakespeare's Text as Construct," *Style* 23 (1989): 335–
51.
   Mowat examines Shakespeare's construction of Theseus as an example of the construction of Shakespearean dramatic character in general. She finds that rather
than being a unitary character "created in a flash of
poetic frenzy," Theseus is "woven from texts [of Ovid,
Chaucer, and Reginald Scot] not only various but rhe-
torically and ideologically at odds." His speeches are
constructed "within a massive field" of printed discourse, including texts "expressing both sides of a

contemporary (and heated) debate" on the imagination and witchcraft.

Nashe, Thomas. *Summer's Last Will and Testament* (1592). In *Thomas Nashe*, ed. Stanley Wells, pp. 91–143. Stratford-upon-Avon Library. London: Edward Arnold, 1964.

Nashe's allegorical play on the theme of summer represents a dramatic style from the early 1590s. In his influential study of Shakespearean comedy, C. L. Barber reads Nashe's drama as analogous to Shakespeare's *Dream*.

Ovid. *The Metamorphoses* (1567). Translated by Arthur Golding. London: Centaur Press, 1961.

Among the direct sources of Shakespeare's works, after North's *Plutarch* and Holinshed's *Chronicles*, probably the most influential was Ovid. In Shakespeare's *Dream* in particular, Ovid's *Metamorphoses* is evident both in the transformation of Bottom and in the play-within-the-play "Pyramus and Thisby." Shakespeare seems to have known Ovid's work in the original Latin and in Arthur Golding's 1567 translation.

Riemer, A. P. *Antic Fables: Patterns of Evasion in Shakespeare's Comedies*. Manchester: Manchester University Press, 1980.

Riemer maintains that modern critical efforts to bring Shakespeare's comedies into line with the dominant tradition of European comedy misunderstands their essential nature. Shakespeare's comic ends, dismissed frequently as too cavalier to be sincere, are for Riemer an assertion that art exists "for the sake of its own conceit [i.e., conception of itself]," and not to castigate folly or correct the manners of the age.

Slights, William W. E. "The Changeling in *A Dream*." *Studies in English Literature* 28 (1988): 259–72.

The disputed changeling boy at the center of Oberon and Titania's custody battle illustrates, for Slights, a principle of indeterminacy evident in many parts of the play. Indeterminacy—that is, contending and conflicted meanings—is the essential condition of people in love, Slight argues. As a figure of indeterminacy, the changeling boy skirts the boundaries between human and other worlds and propels the play into the "uncharted territory on the fringes or 'margins' of society" where rules of power collapse, leading to liberating and amusing results.

Shakespeare's Language

Abbott, E. A. *A Shakespearian Grammar.* New York: Haskell House, 1972.

This compact reference book, first published in 1870, helps with many difficulties in Shakespeare's language. It systematically accounts for a host of differences between Shakespeare's usage and sentence structure and our own.

Blake, Norman. *Shakespeare's Language: An Introduction.* New York: St. Martin's Press, 1983.

This general introduction to Elizabethan English discusses various aspects of the language of Shakespeare and his contemporaries, offering possible meanings for hundreds of ambiguous constructions.

Dobson, E. J. *English Pronunciation, 1500–1700.* 2 vols. Oxford: Clarendon Press, 1968.

This long and technical work includes chapters on spelling (and its reformation), phonetics, stressed vowels, and consonants in early modern English.

Houston, John. *Shakespearean Sentences: A Study in Style and Syntax.* Baton Rouge: Louisiana State University Press, 1988.

Houston studies Shakespeare's stylistic choices, considering matters such as sentence length and the relative positions of subject, verb, and direct object. Examining plays throughout the canon in a roughly chronological, developmental order, he analyzes how sentence structure is used in setting tone, in characterization, and for other dramatic purposes.

Onions, C. T. *A Shakespeare Glossary.* Oxford: Clarendon Press, 1986.

This revised edition updates Onions's standard, selective glossary of words and phrases in Shakespeare's plays that are now obsolete, archaic, or obscure.

Partridge, Eric. *Shakespeare's Bawdy.* London: Routledge & Kegan Paul, 1955.

After an introductory essay, "The Sexual, the Homosexual, and Non-Sexual Bawdy in Shakespeare," Partridge provides a comprehensive glossary of "bawdy" phrases and words from the plays.

Robinson, Randal. *Unlocking Shakespeare's Language: Help for the Teacher and Student.* Urbana, Ill.: National Council of Teachers of English and the ERIC Clearinghouse on Reading and Communication Skills, 1989.

Specifically designed for the high-school and undergraduate college teacher and student, Robinson's book addresses the problems that most often hinder present-day readers of Shakespeare. Through work with his own students, Robinson found that many readers today are particularly puzzled by such stylistic characteristics as subject-verb inversion, interrupted structures, and compression. He shows how our own colloquial language contains comparable structures, and thus helps students recognize such structures when they find them in Shakespeare's plays. This book supplies worksheets—with examples from major plays—to illuminate and remedy such problems as unusual sequences of words and the separation of related parts of sentences.

Shakespeare's Life

Baldwin, T. W. *William Shakspere's Petty School.* Urbana: University of Illinois Press, 1943.

Baldwin here investigates the theory and practice of the petty school, the first level of education in Elizabethan England. He focuses on that educational system primarily as it is reflected in Shakespeare's art.

Baldwin, T. W. *William Shakspere's Small Latine and Lesse Greeke.* 2 vols. Urbana: University of Illinois Press, 1944.

Baldwin attacks the view that Shakespeare was an uneducated genius—a view that had been dominant among Shakespeareans since the eighteenth century. Instead, Baldwin shows, the educational system of Shakespeare's time would have given the playwright a strong background in the classics, and there is much in the plays that shows how Shakespeare benefited from such an education.

Beier, A. L., and Roger Finlay, eds. *London 1500–1700: The Making of the Metropolis.* New York: Longman, 1986.

Focusing on the economic and social history of early modern London, these collected essays probe aspects of metropolitan life, including "Population and Disease," "Commerce and Manufacture," and "Society and Change."

Bentley, G. E. *Shakespeare's Life: A Biographical Handbook.* New Haven: Yale University Press, 1961.

This "just-the-facts" account presents the surviving documents of Shakespeare's life against an Elizabethan background.

Chambers, E. K. *William Shakespeare: A Study of Facts and Problems.* 2 vols. Oxford: Clarendon Press, 1930.

Analyzing in great detail the scant historical data, Chambers's complex, scholarly study considers the nature of the texts in which Shakespeare's work is preserved.

Cressy, David. *Education in Tudor and Stuart England.* London: Edward Arnold, 1975.

This volume collects sixteenth-, seventeenth-, and early-eighteenth-century documents detailing aspects of formal education in England, such as the curriculum, the control and organization of education, and the education of women.

Dutton, Richard. *William Shakespeare: A Literary Life.* New York: St. Martin's Press, 1989.

Not a biography in the traditional sense, Dutton's very readable work nevertheless "follows the contours of Shakespeare's life" as he examines Shakespeare's career as playwright and poet, with consideration of his patrons, theatrical associations, and audience.

Fraser, Russell. *Young Shakespeare.* New York: Columbia University Press, 1988.

Fraser focuses on Shakespeare's first thirty years, paying attention simultaneously to his life and art.

De Grazia, Margreta. *Shakespeare Verbatim: The Reproduction of Authenticity and the Apparatus of 1790.* Oxford: Clarendon Press, 1991.

De Grazia traces and discusses the development of

such editorial criteria as authenticity, historical period-
ization, factual biography, chronological developments,
and close reading, locating as the point of origin Ed-
mond Malone's 1790 edition of Shakespeare's works.
There are interesting chapters on the First Folio and
on the "legendary" versus the "documented" Shakespeare.

Schoenbaum, S. *William Shakespeare: A Compact Documentary Life*. New York: Oxford University Press, 1977.
   This standard biography economically presents the
essential documents from Shakespeare's time in an
accessible narrative account of the playwright's life.

Shakespeare's Theater

Bentley, G. E. *The Profession of Player in Shakespeare's
Time, 1590–1642*. Princeton: Princeton University Press,
1984.
   Bentley readably sets forth a wealth of evidence about
performance in Shakespeare's time, with special attention to the relations between player and company, and
the business of casting, managing, and touring.

Berry, Herbert. *Shakespeare's Playhouses*. New York:
AMS Press, 1987.
   Berry's six essays collected here discuss (with illustra-
tions) varying aspects of the four playhouses in which
Shakespeare had a financial stake: the Theatre in
Shoreditch, the Blackfriars, and the first and second
Globe.

Cook, Ann Jennalie. *The Privileged Playgoers of Shakespeare's London*. Princeton: Princeton University Press,
1981.

Cook's work argues, on the basis of sociological, economic, and documentary evidence, that Shakespeare's audience—and the audience for English Renaissance drama generally—consisted mainly of the "privileged."

Greg, W. W. *Dramatic Documents from the Elizabethan Playhouses.* 2 vols. Oxford: Clarendon Press, 1931.

Greg itemizes and briefly describes almost all the play manuscripts that survive from the period 1590 to around 1660, including, among other things, players' parts. His second volume offers facsimiles of selected manuscripts.

Gurr, Andrew. *Playgoing in Shakespeare's London.* Cambridge: Cambridge University Press, 1987.

Gurr charts how the theatrical enterprise developed from its modest beginnings in the late 1560s to become a thriving institution in the 1600s. He argues that there were important changes over the period 1567–1644 in the playhouses, the audience, and the plays.

Harbage, Alfred. *Shakespeare's Audience.* New York: Columbia University Press, 1941.

Harbage investigates the fragmentary surviving evidence to interpret the size, composition, and behavior of Shakespeare's audience.

Hattaway, Michael. *Elizabethan Popular Theatre: Plays in Performance.* London: Routledge & Kegan Paul, 1982.

Beginning with a study of the popular drama of the late Elizabethan age—a description of the stages, performance conditions, and acting of the period—this volume concludes with an analysis of five well-known plays of the 1590s, one of them (*Titus Andronicus*) by Shakespeare.

Shapiro, Michael. *Children of the Revels: The Boy Compa-nies of Shakespeare's Time and Their Plays*. New York: Columbia University Press, 1977.

Shapiro chronicles the history of the amateur and quasi-professional child companies that flourished in London at the end of Elizabeth's reign and the begin-ning of James's.

The Publication of Shakespeare's Plays

Blayney, Peter. *The First Folio of Shakespeare*. Hanover, Md.: Folger, 1991.

Blayney's accessible account of the printing and later life of the First Folio—an amply illustrated catalogue to a 1991 Folger Shakespeare Library exhibition—analyzes the mechanical production of the First Folio, describing how the Folio was made, by whom and for whom, how much it cost, and its ups and downs (or, rather, downs and ups) since its printing in 1623.

Hinman, Charlton. *The Printing and Proof-Reading of the First Folio of Shakespeare*. 2 vols. Oxford: Clarendon Press, 1963.

In the most arduous study of a single book ever undertaken, Hinman attempts to reconstruct how the Shakespeare First Folio of 1623 was set into type and run off the press, sheet by sheet. He also provides almost all the known variations in readings from copy to copy.

Hinman, Charlton. *The Norton Facsimile: The First Folio of Shakespeare*. New York: W. W. Norton, 1968.

This facsimile presents a photographic reproduction of an "ideal" copy of the First Folio of Shakespeare; Hinman attempts to represent each page in its most fully corrected state.

Key To
Famous Lines and Phrases

The course of true love never did run smooth.
[Lysander—1.1.136]

Over hill, over dale . . .   [Fairy—2.1.2 ff.]

Ill met by moonlight, proud Titania. [Oberon—2.1.62]

. . . a fair vestal thronèd by the west
[Oberon—2.1.164]

In maiden meditation, fancy-free   [Oberon—2.1.170]

I'll put a girdle round about the earth . . .
[Robin—2.1.181]

I know a bank where the wild thyme blows . . .
[Oberon—2.1.257]

You spotted snakes with double tongue . . .
[First Fairy—2.2.9 ff.]

Lord, what fools these mortals be!   [Robin—3.2.117]

I was with Hercules and Cadmus once,
When in a wood of Crete they bayed the bear . . .
[Hippolyta—4.1.116–17]

The lunatic, the lover, and the poet
Are of imagination all compact.   [Theseus—5.1.7–8]

The lover . . .
Sees Helen's beauty in a brow of Egypt.
[Theseus—5.1.10–11]